How To Read
HTML Code For E-Books

How To Read HTML Code For E-Books

BY

TRACY WILSON

http://beautifulpublications.com

Published by
Beautiful Publications LLC
Stratford, CT 06614

LIBRARY OF CONGRESS CONTROL NUMBER: 2021913845

PRINT ISBN: 978-1-7373828-2-9
EBOOK ISBN: 978-1-7373828-3-6

Printed in the United States of America

This book is dedicated to everyone that got frustrated and got a headache trying to fix an e-book.

Contents

INTRODUCTION

All you wanted to do was turn your story into a beautiful publication. You read my book. You wrote your story. You sent your book off to be formatted. You uploaded your e-book to amazon and it wasn't aligned. It wasn't indented where it should've been indented. You have 1, 2, 3, and 4 where you wanted a, b, c, and d. You have no idea how to fix it, you're frustrated, and you have a headache. Before you throw your computer out the window, continue reading.

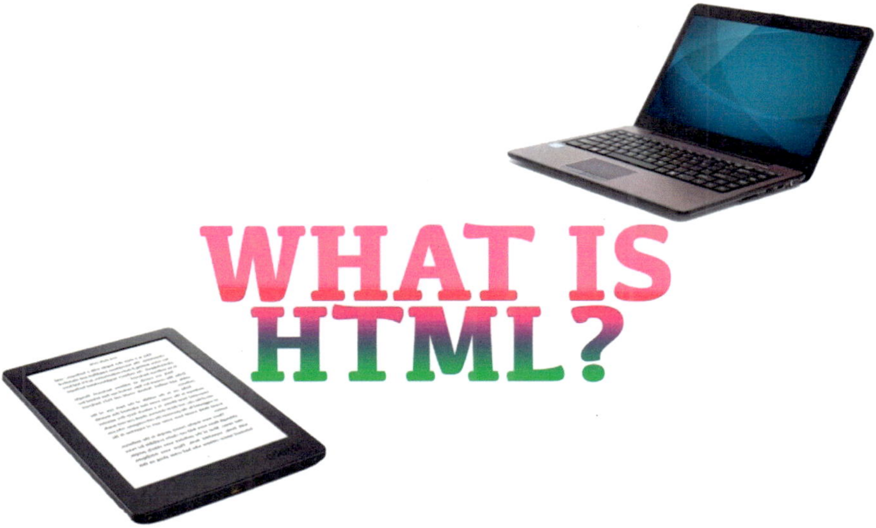

HTML = Hyper Text Markup Language. HTML tells your computer, kindle, nook, or tablet how to display your photos and text.

MY EXPERIENCE

I got experience reading and adjusting html when I ran spades and backgammon tournaments in the MSN Gaming Zone. The other directors would have these fancy pages and backgrounds and I wanted to create my own so I asked them how they did it. Once I learned how to create the pages using html, I would save them and whenever I wanted to create a new page, I'd open up a page that was already done and make adjustments to it so I didn't have to re-create everything from scratch.

I got experience reading and adjusting html code for e-books after I published my first e-book. I would open calibre, add my book, and look at the html code. Most of the time I didn't need to read it to fix anything but typos; however, after I saw how my book, Turn Your Story Into A Beautiful Publication, looked in calibre, I had to try and fix it.

I got frustrated, I got headaches, and I vented, but I didn't give up. It took me staying up until nearly 4 a.m. some nights into mornings – but when I figured out how to fix it, I was so happy!

I wrote this book to save you time, keep you from getting aggravated, keep you from losing sleep, keep you from getting headaches, help you fix your e-book, and teach you how to read html codes.

WHY DO I NEED TO EDIT MY E-BOOK?

No software is perfect. Every program isn't perfectly compatible with every other program. When it comes to writing, there are programs that are only available for Mac, just as there are programs that are only available for Microsoft. Before I wrote this book, I learned that if you want your book on more than one platform, you will need a kindle version as well as a generic version.

OPENING YOUR E-BOOK IN CALIBRE

The first thing you need to do is open your e-book in calibre. If you don't have calibre, go to their website at http://calibre-ebook.com and download it to your computer.

1. Open calibre.
2. Click okay to add your book.
3. Right-click on your book, scroll down to edit, and click on edit.

Once you open your e-book in calibre, you'll see 3 screens:

1. Page Titles
2. HTML Code
3. What your book will look like on an e-reader.

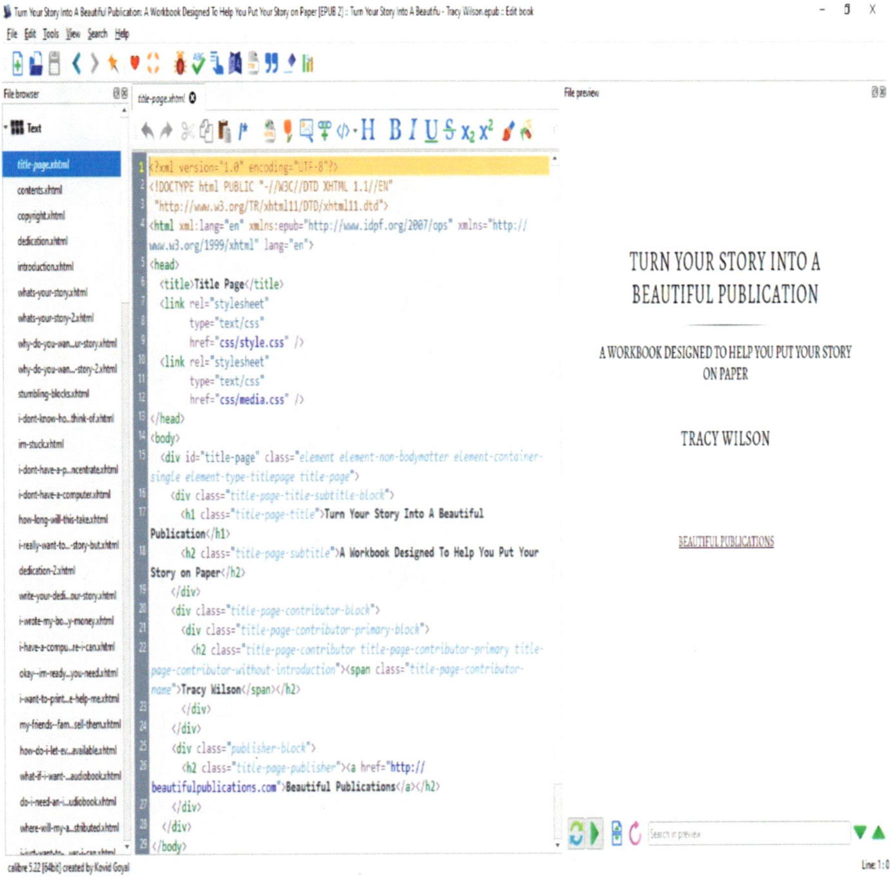

Click on each page and scroll through your e-book. Use the mouse to scroll down the html code. As you scroll through the html code, pay attention to words or characters underlined in red. If there are any miss-spelled words, you can click inside the html code and correct them. Once you correct them, you'll see your corrections to the right. If you are okay with your corrections, click on the disk at the top-left of your screen and save it.

FIXING THE HTML CODE

When I got my e-book back, I scrolled through my book and I saw the following:

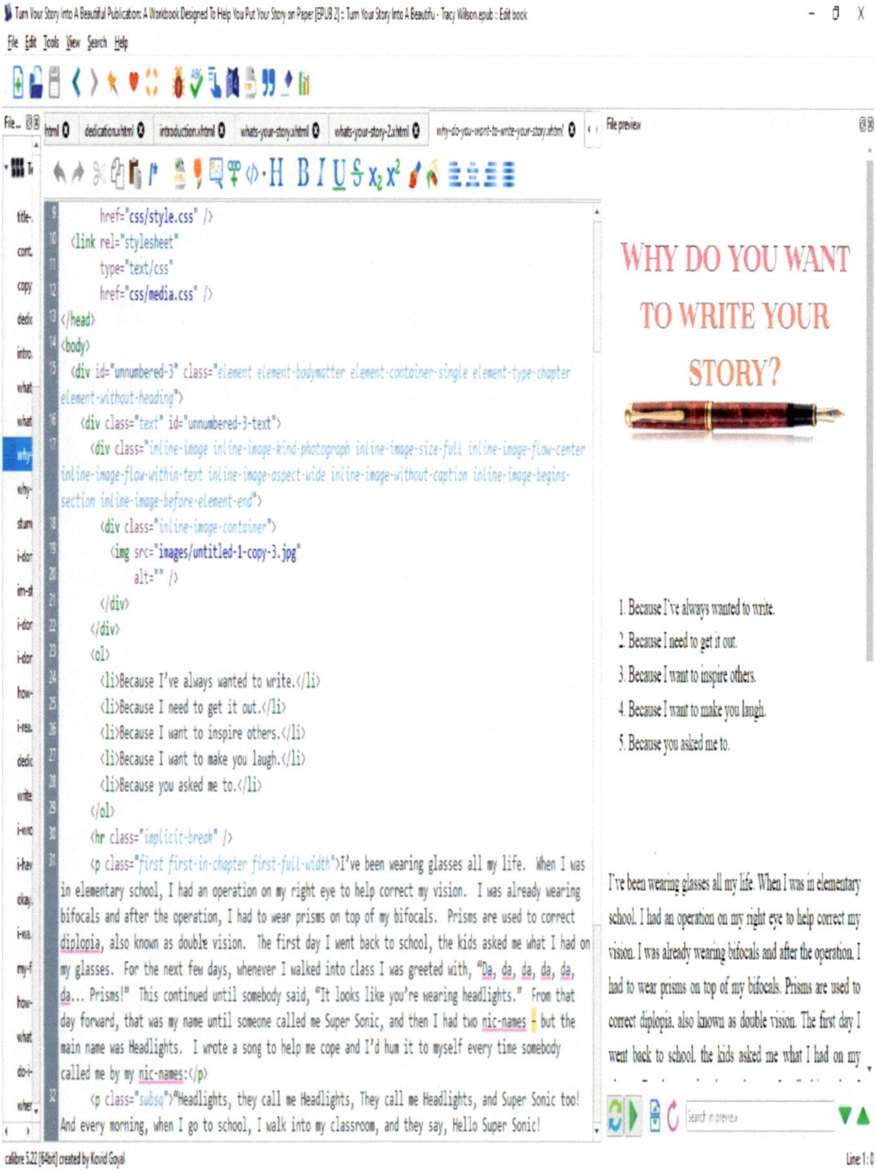
Turn Your Story into A Beautiful Publication: A Workbook Designed To Help You Put Your Story on Paper [EPUB 2] :: Turn Your Story Into A Beautifu - Tracy Wilson.epub :: Edit book
File Edit Tools View Search Help
dedication.xhtml
introduction.xhtml
whats-your-story.xhtml
whats-your-story-2.xhtml
why-do-you-want-to-write-your-story.xhtml
File preview
href="css/style.css" />
<link rel="stylesheet"
type="text/css"
href="css/media.css" />
</head>
<body>
<div id="unnumbered-3" class="element element-bodymatter element-container-single element-type-chapter element-without-heading">
<div class="text" id="unnumbered-3-text">
<div class="inline-image inline-image-kind-photograph inline-image-size-full inline-image-flow-center inline-image-flow-within-text inline-image-aspect-wide inline-image-without-caption inline-image-begins-section inline-image-before-element-end">
<div class="inline-image-container">
<img src="images/untitled-1-copy-3.jpg"
alt="" />
</div>
</div>
<ol>
<li>Because I've always wanted to write.</li>
<li>Because I need to get it out.</li>
<li>Because I want to inspire others.</li>
<li>Because I want to make you laugh.</li>
<li>Because you asked me to.</li>
</ol>
<hr class="implicit-break" />
<p class="first first-in-chapter first-full-width">I've been wearing glasses all my life. When I was in elementary school, I had an operation on my right eye to help correct my vision. I was already wearing bifocals and after the operation, I had to wear prisms on top of my bifocals. Prisms are used to correct diplopia, also known as double vision. The first day I went back to school, the kids asked me what I had on my glasses. For the next few days, whenever I walked into class I was greeted with, "Da, da, da, da, da, da... Prisms!" This continued until somebody said, "It looks like you're wearing headlights." From that day forward, that was my name until someone called me Super Sonic, and then I had two nic-names - but the main name was Headlights. I wrote a song to help me cope and I'd hum it to myself every time somebody called me by my nic-names:</p>
<p class="subsq">"Headlights, they call me Headlights, They call me Headlights, and Super Sonic too! And every morning, when I go to school, I walk into my classroom, and they say, Hello Super Sonic!
WHY DO YOU WANT TO WRITE YOUR STORY?
1. Because I've always wanted to write.
2. Because I need to get it out.
3. Because I want to inspire others.
4. Because I want to make you laugh.
5. Because you asked me to.
I've been wearing glasses all my life. When I was in elementary school. I had an operation on my right eye to help correct my vision. I was already wearing bifocals and after the operation, I had to wear prisms on top of my bifocals. Prisms are used to correct diplopia, also known as double vision. The first day I went back to school, the kids asked me what I had on my
Search in preview
calibre 5.22 [64bit] created by Kovid Goyal
Line 1: 0

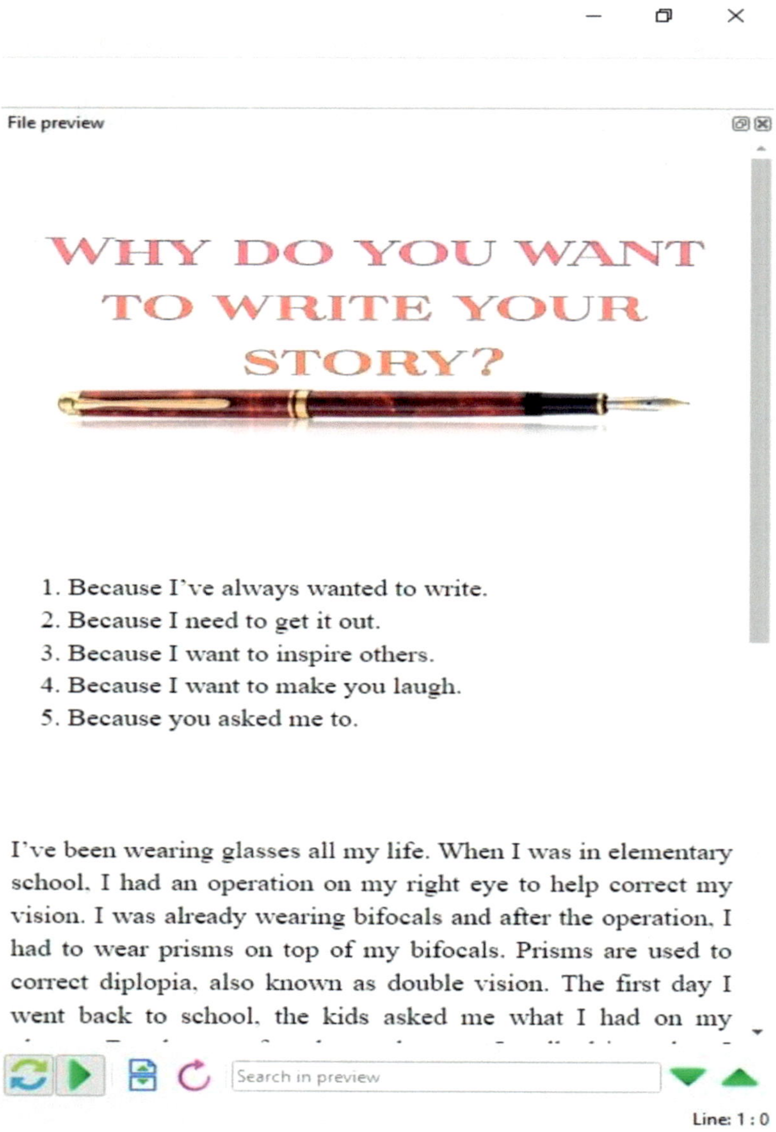
File preview
WHY DO YOU WANT TO WRITE YOUR STORY?
1. Because I've always wanted to write.
2. Because I need to get it out.
3. Because I want to inspire others.
4. Because I want to make you laugh.
5. Because you asked me to.
I've been wearing glasses all my life. When I was in elementary school, I had an operation on my right eye to help correct my vision. I was already wearing bifocals and after the operation, I had to wear prisms on top of my bifocals. Prisms are used to correct diplopia, also known as double vision. The first day I went back to school, the kids asked me what I had on my
Search in preview
Line: 1 : 0

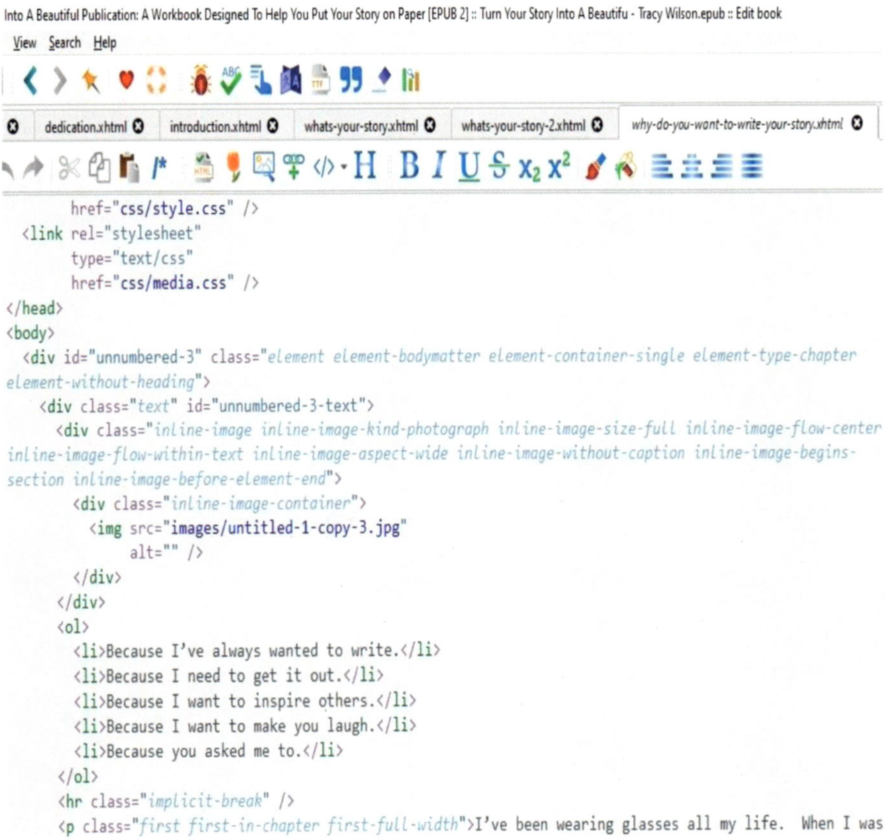

The html code in the picture has <li> before and </li> after each line so instead of having a, b, c, d, e, I had 1, 2, 3, 4, 5. This is what I did to fix it:

I left the <ol> at the top of the <li> section because that tells the html to indent. I removed the <li> in front of each line and replaced it with a, b, c, d, e. I also removed the </li> after each line and replaced it with <p>. This tells html to put each entry on a separate line. Once I did that, I had the look I wanted and saved it:

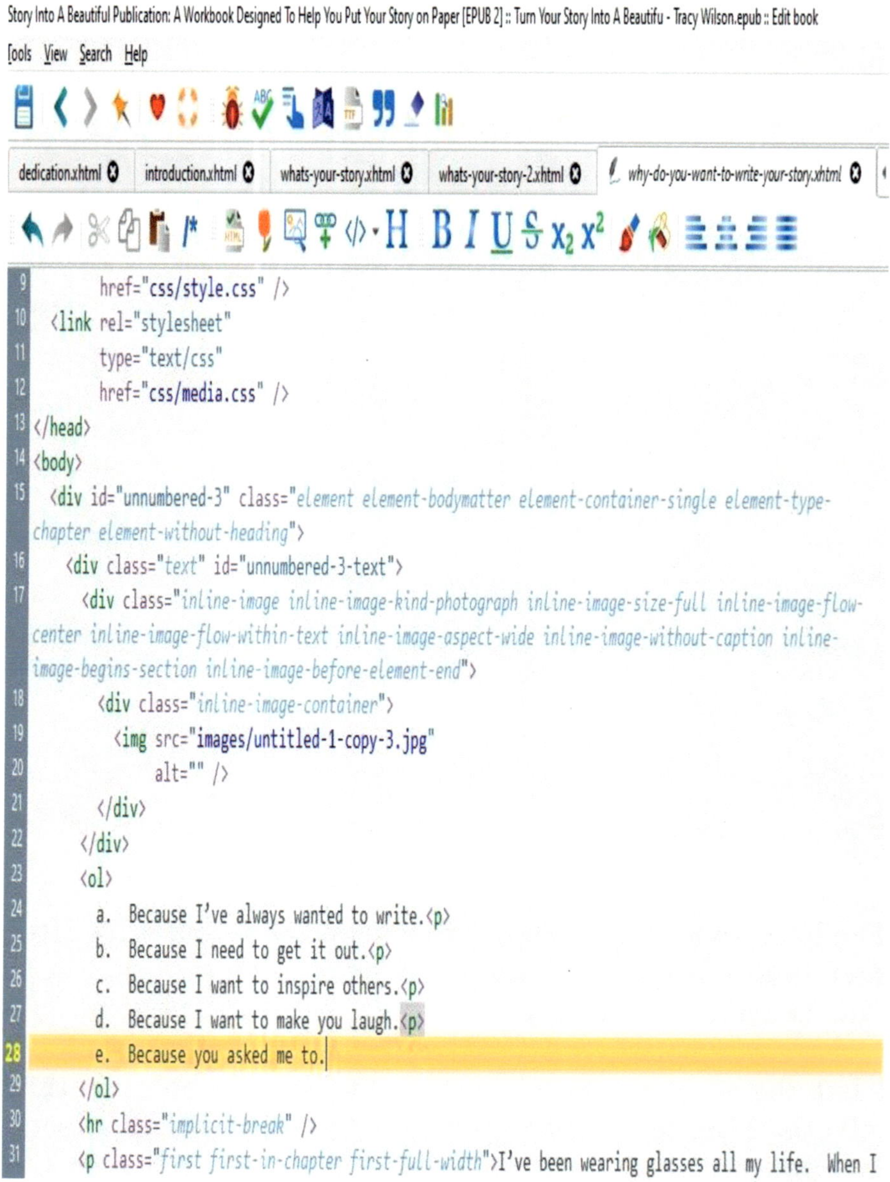
Story Into A Beautiful Publication: A Workbook Designed To Help You Put Your Story on Paper [EPUB 2] :: Turn Your Story Into A Beautifu - Tracy Wilson.epub :: Edit book
Tools View Search Help
dedication.xhtml
introduction.xhtml
whats-your-story.xhtml
whats-your-story-2.xhtml
why-do-you-want-to-write-your-story.xhtml
href="css/style.css" />
<link rel="stylesheet"
type="text/css"
href="css/media.css" />
</head>
<body>
<div id="unnumbered-3" class="element element-bodymatter element-container-single element-type-chapter element-without-heading">
<div class="text" id="unnumbered-3-text">
<div class="inline-image inline-image-kind-photograph inline-image-size-full inline-image-flow-center inline-image-flow-within-text inline-image-aspect-wide inline-image-without-caption inline-image-begins-section inline-image-before-element-end">
<div class="inline-image-container">
<img src="images/untitled-1-copy-3.jpg"
alt="" />
</div>
</div>
<ol>
a. Because I've always wanted to write.<p>
b. Because I need to get it out.<p>
c. Because I want to inspire others.<p>
d. Because I want to make you laugh.<p>
e. Because you asked me to.
</ol>
<hr class="implicit-break" />
<p class="first first-in-chapter first-full-width">I've been wearing glasses all my life. When I

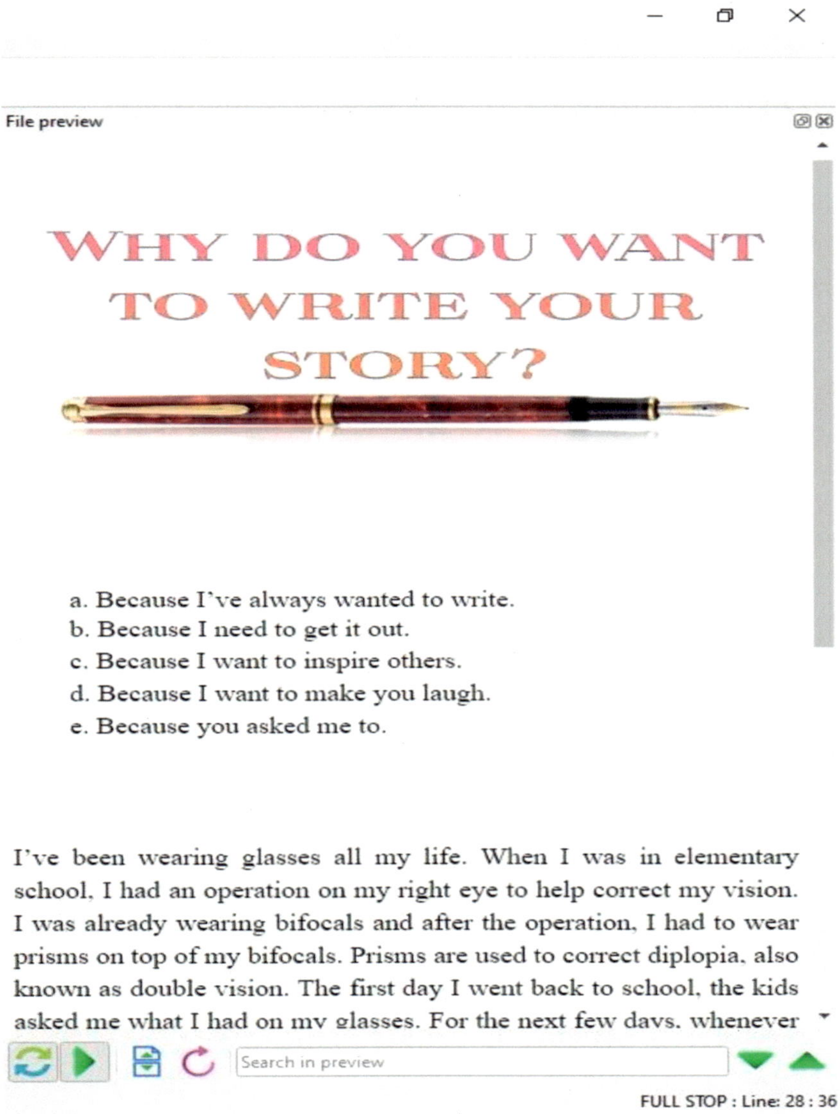
File preview
WHY DO YOU WANT TO WRITE YOUR STORY?
a. Because I've always wanted to write.
b. Because I need to get it out.
c. Because I want to inspire others.
d. Because I want to make you laugh.
e. Because you asked me to.
I've been wearing glasses all my life. When I was in elementary school, I had an operation on my right eye to help correct my vision. I was already wearing bifocals and after the operation, I had to wear prisms on top of my bifocals. Prisms are used to correct diplopia, also known as double vision. The first day I went back to school, the kids asked me what I had on my glasses. For the next few days, whenever
Search in preview
FULL STOP : Line: 28 : 36

When I got to 'Stumbling Blocks' I saw the following:

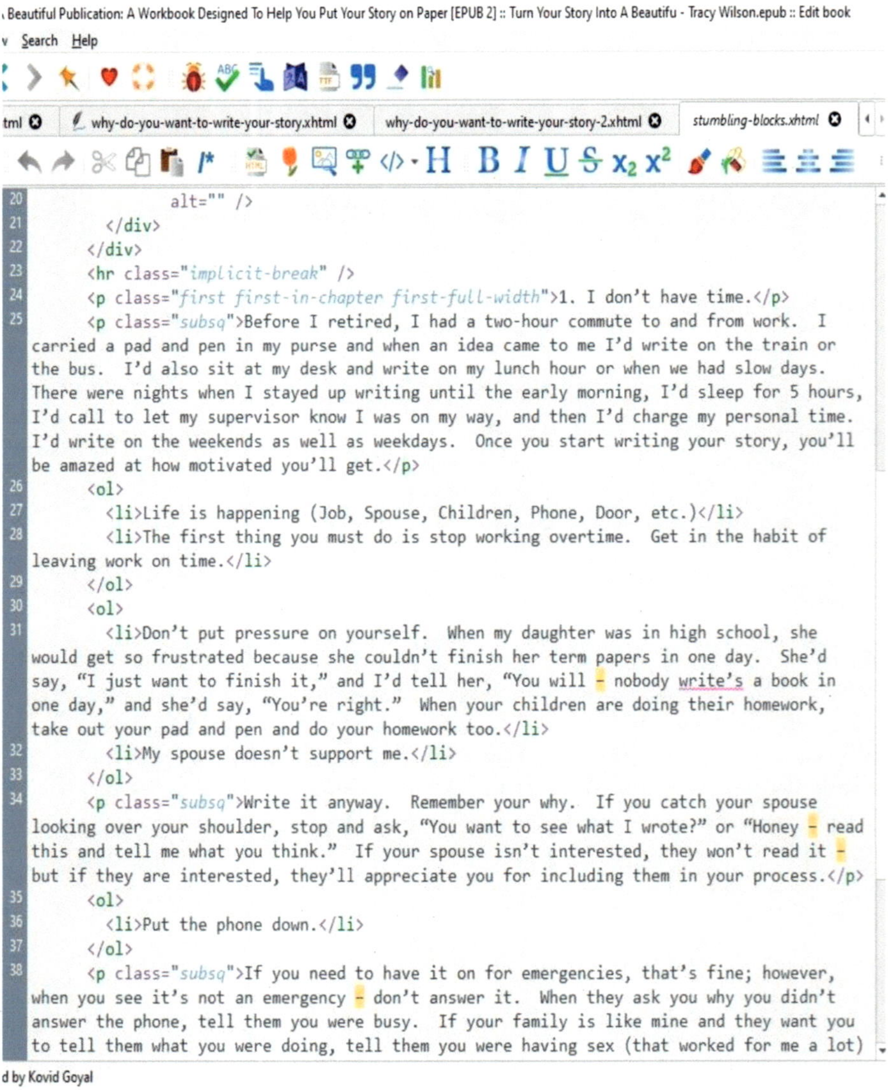


```
                alt="" />
        </div>
      </div>
      <hr class="implicit-break" />
      <p class="first first-in-chapter first-full-width">1. I don't have time.</p>
      <p class="subsq">Before I retired, I had a two-hour commute to and from work.  I carried a pad and pen in my purse and when an idea came to me I'd write on the train or the bus.  I'd also sit at my desk and write on my lunch hour or when we had slow days.  There were nights when I stayed up writing until the early morning, I'd sleep for 5 hours, I'd call to let my supervisor know I was on my way, and then I'd charge my personal time.  I'd write on the weekends as well as weekdays.  Once you start writing your story, you'll be amazed at how motivated you'll get.</p>
      <ol>
        <li>Life is happening (Job, Spouse, Children, Phone, Door, etc.)</li>
        <li>The first thing you must do is stop working overtime.  Get in the habit of leaving work on time.</li>
      </ol>
      <ol>
        <li>Don't put pressure on yourself.  When my daughter was in high school, she would get so frustrated because she couldn't finish her term papers in one day.  She'd say, "I just want to finish it," and I'd tell her, "You will - nobody write's a book in one day," and she'd say, "You're right."  When your children are doing their homework, take out your pad and pen and do your homework too.</li>
        <li>My spouse doesn't support me.</li>
      </ol>
      <p class="subsq">Write it anyway.  Remember your why.  If you catch your spouse looking over your shoulder, stop and ask, "You want to see what I wrote?" or "Honey - read this and tell me what you think."  If your spouse isn't interested, they won't read it - but if they are interested, they'll appreciate you for including them in your process.</p>
      <ol>
        <li>Put the phone down.</li>
      </ol>
      <p class="subsq">If you need to have it on for emergencies, that's fine; however, when you see it's not an emergency - don't answer it.  When they ask you why you didn't answer the phone, tell them you were busy.  If your family is like mine and they want you to tell them what you were doing, tell them you were having sex (that worked for me a lot)
```

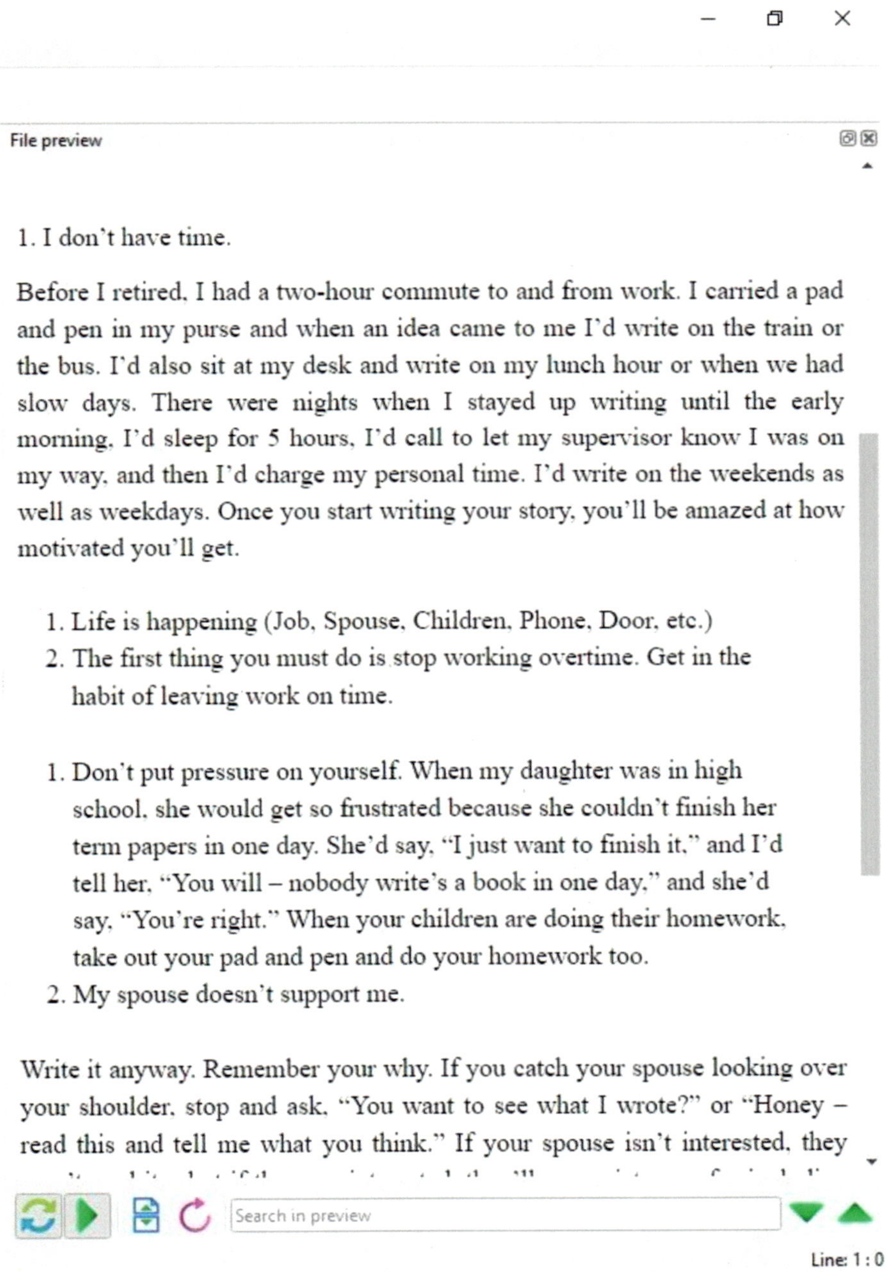

File preview

1. I don't have time.

Before I retired, I had a two-hour commute to and from work. I carried a pad and pen in my purse and when an idea came to me I'd write on the train or the bus. I'd also sit at my desk and write on my lunch hour or when we had slow days. There were nights when I stayed up writing until the early morning, I'd sleep for 5 hours, I'd call to let my supervisor know I was on my way, and then I'd charge my personal time. I'd write on the weekends as well as weekdays. Once you start writing your story, you'll be amazed at how motivated you'll get.

1. Life is happening (Job, Spouse, Children, Phone, Door, etc.)
2. The first thing you must do is stop working overtime. Get in the habit of leaving work on time.

1. Don't put pressure on yourself. When my daughter was in high school, she would get so frustrated because she couldn't finish her term papers in one day. She'd say, "I just want to finish it," and I'd tell her, "You will – nobody write's a book in one day," and she'd say, "You're right." When your children are doing their homework, take out your pad and pen and do your homework too.
2. My spouse doesn't support me.

Write it anyway. Remember your why. If you catch your spouse looking over your shoulder, stop and ask, "You want to see what I wrote?" or "Honey – read this and tell me what you think." If your spouse isn't interested, they

This had me stumped. I wanted 1, 2, a, b, 3, but instead I had 1, 1, 2, 1, 2. The first thing I did was correct the miss-spelled word I saw underlined, write's. After I corrected that and saved it, I went to work on the Stumbling Blocks.

1. I changed the </p> after I don't have time to </ol> because I wanted a space between the first line and the paragraph.

2. I copied <hr class="implicit-break"></p> to where line 2 began and then I changed the beginning from hr to p: <p class="implicit-break"</p>.

3. I copied the html code underneath that line after that and pasted it in front of where line 2 was going to begin: <p class="first first-in-chapter first-full-width">.

4. I changed the </li> at the end of line 2 to </p>.

5. I copied <p class="subsq"> and changed <li> to <ol>: <p class="subsq"><ol> and typed a. in front of The first thing you must do, and then I removed <li> at the end of the line and changed it to </ol>.

6. I copied <p class="subsq"><ol> to the next line and typed b. in front of don't put pressure on yourself and then I changed <li> to </ol>. This put a space between 2b and 3.

7. I removed <li> from in front of 'My spouse doesn't support me,' I removed the </li>at the end, kept the </ol>, and typed 3. in front of the words.

8. I copied <p class="subsq"> in front of 'Write it anyway' and put </ol> at the end of the paragraph.

9. I copied <p class="implicit-break"></p> and <p class="first first-in-chapter first-full-width">, typed 4. in front of Put the phone down, and typed </ol> at the end of the line.

10. I copied <p class="implicit-break"></p> and <p class="first first-in-chapter first-full-width">, typed 5. In front of Don't answer the door unless you have to, and removed </li> at the end of the line.

After I completed those ten steps, my html code and e-book looked like I wanted it to:

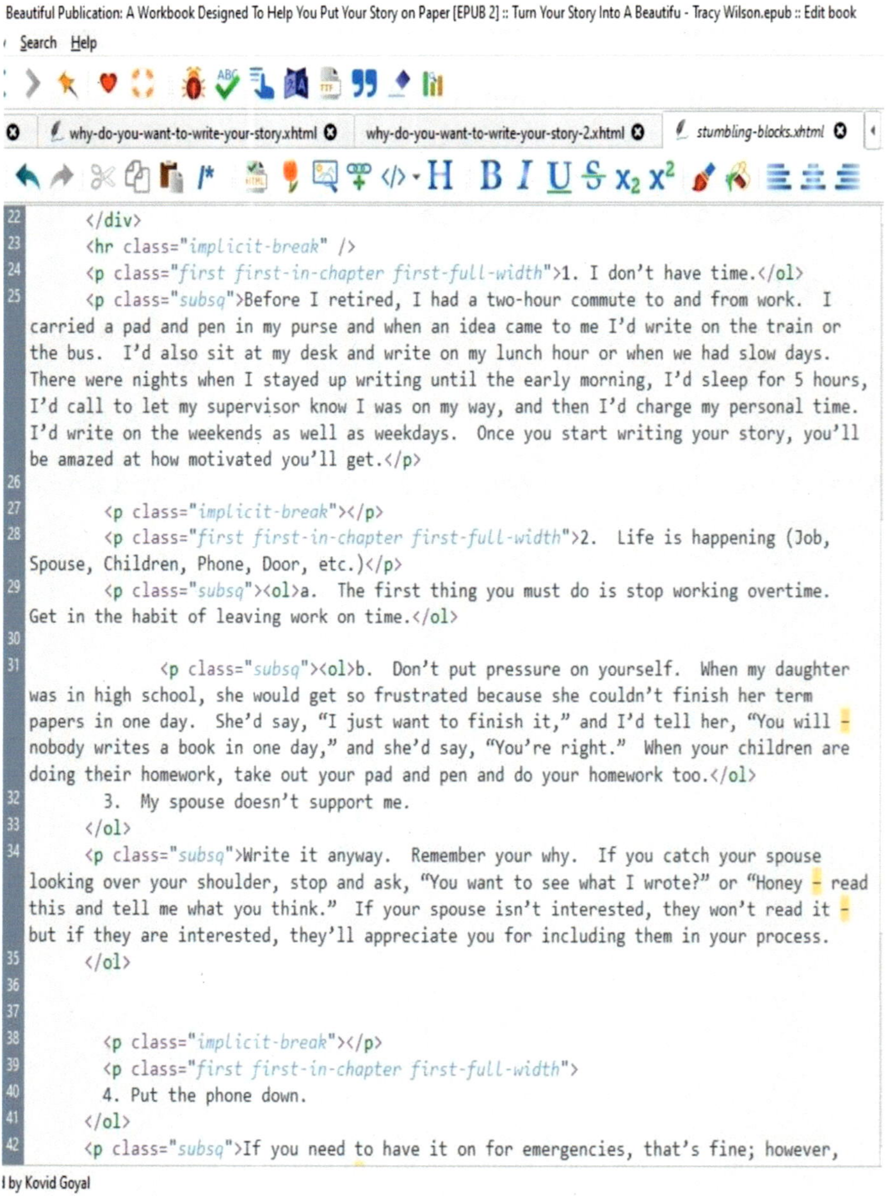


```
      </div>
      <hr class="implicit-break" />
      <p class="first first-in-chapter first-full-width">1. I don't have time.</ol>
      <p class="subsq">Before I retired, I had a two-hour commute to and from work.  I carried a pad and pen in my purse and when an idea came to me I'd write on the train or the bus.  I'd also sit at my desk and write on my lunch hour or when we had slow days.  There were nights when I stayed up writing until the early morning, I'd sleep for 5 hours, I'd call to let my supervisor know I was on my way, and then I'd charge my personal time.  I'd write on the weekends as well as weekdays.  Once you start writing your story, you'll be amazed at how motivated you'll get.</p>

        <p class="implicit-break"></p>
        <p class="first first-in-chapter first-full-width">2.  Life is happening (Job, Spouse, Children, Phone, Door, etc.)</p>
        <p class="subsq"><ol>a.  The first thing you must do is stop working overtime.  Get in the habit of leaving work on time.</ol>

              <p class="subsq"><ol>b.  Don't put pressure on yourself.  When my daughter was in high school, she would get so frustrated because she couldn't finish her term papers in one day.  She'd say, "I just want to finish it," and I'd tell her, "You will - nobody writes a book in one day," and she'd say, "You're right."  When your children are doing their homework, take out your pad and pen and do your homework too.</ol>
        3.  My spouse doesn't support me.
      </ol>
      <p class="subsq">Write it anyway.  Remember your why.  If you catch your spouse looking over your shoulder, stop and ask, "You want to see what I wrote?" or "Honey - read this and tell me what you think."  If your spouse isn't interested, they won't read it - but if they are interested, they'll appreciate you for including them in your process.
      </ol>



        <p class="implicit-break"></p>
        <p class="first first-in-chapter first-full-width">
        4. Put the phone down.
      </ol>
      <p class="subsq">If you need to have it on for emergencies, that's fine; however,
```

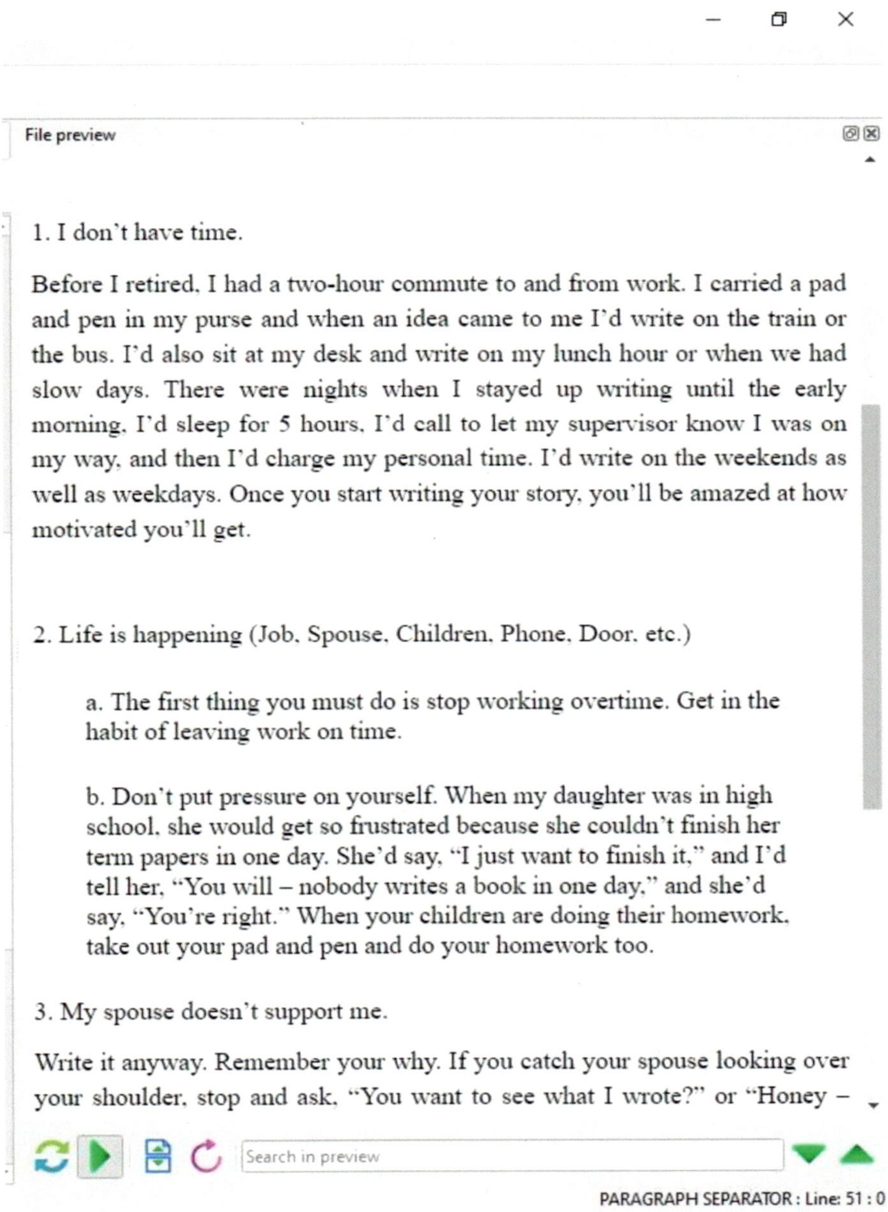

1. I don't have time.

Before I retired, I had a two-hour commute to and from work. I carried a pad and pen in my purse and when an idea came to me I'd write on the train or the bus. I'd also sit at my desk and write on my lunch hour or when we had slow days. There were nights when I stayed up writing until the early morning. I'd sleep for 5 hours, I'd call to let my supervisor know I was on my way, and then I'd charge my personal time. I'd write on the weekends as well as weekdays. Once you start writing your story, you'll be amazed at how motivated you'll get.

2. Life is happening (Job, Spouse, Children, Phone, Door, etc.)

a. The first thing you must do is stop working overtime. Get in the habit of leaving work on time.

b. Don't put pressure on yourself. When my daughter was in high school, she would get so frustrated because she couldn't finish her term papers in one day. She'd say, "I just want to finish it," and I'd tell her, "You will – nobody writes a book in one day," and she'd say, "You're right." When your children are doing their homework, take out your pad and pen and do your homework too.

3. My spouse doesn't support me.

Write it anyway. Remember your why. If you catch your spouse looking over your shoulder, stop and ask, "You want to see what I wrote?" or "Honey –

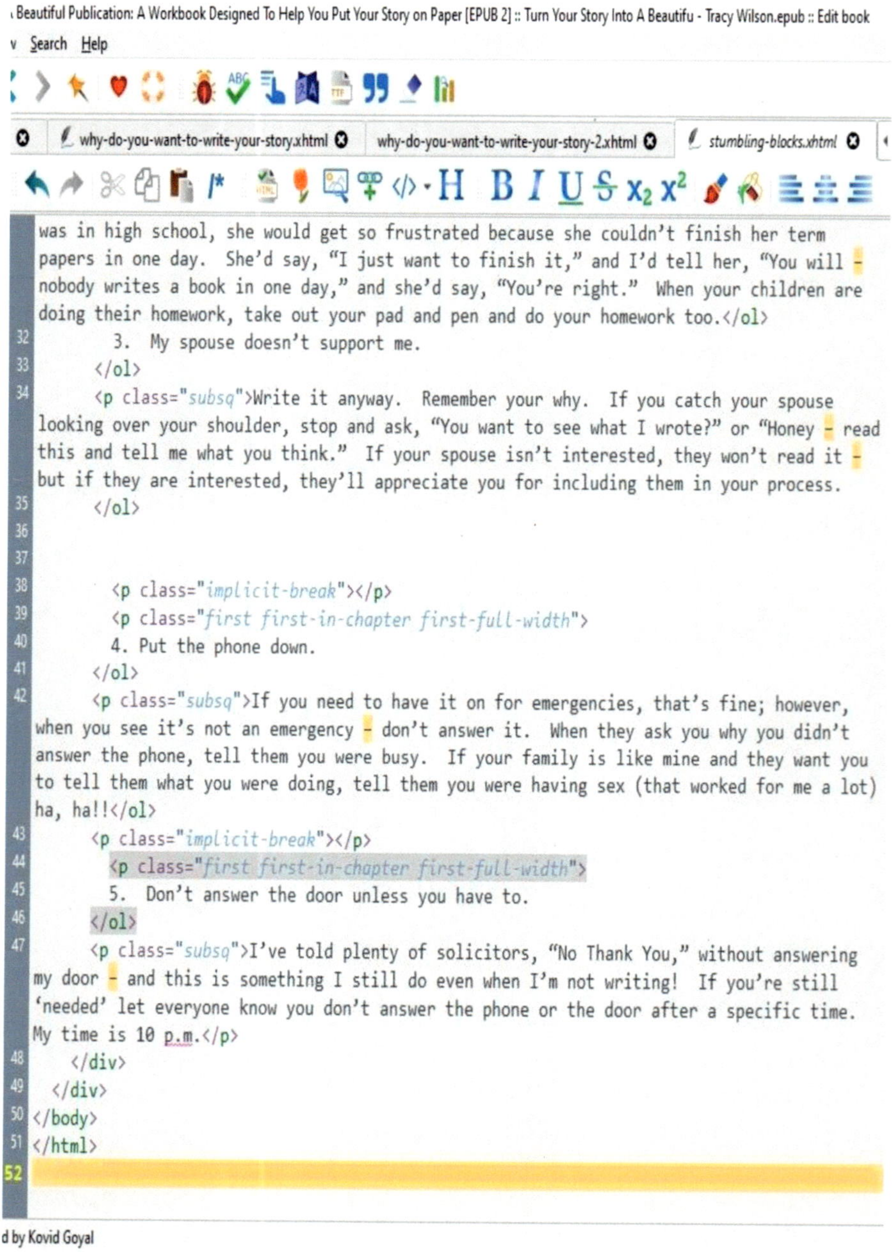


```
was in high school, she would get so frustrated because she couldn’t finish her term papers in one day.  She’d say, “I just want to finish it,” and I’d tell her, “You will - nobody writes a book in one day,” and she’d say, “You’re right.”  When your children are doing their homework, take out your pad and pen and do your homework too.</ol>
        3.  My spouse doesn’t support me.
      </ol>
      <p class="subsq">Write it anyway.  Remember your why.  If you catch your spouse looking over your shoulder, stop and ask, “You want to see what I wrote?” or “Honey - read this and tell me what you think.”  If your spouse isn’t interested, they won’t read it - but if they are interested, they’ll appreciate you for including them in your process.
      </ol>



        <p class="implicit-break"></p>
        <p class="first first-in-chapter first-full-width">
        4. Put the phone down.
      </ol>
      <p class="subsq">If you need to have it on for emergencies, that’s fine; however, when you see it’s not an emergency - don’t answer it.  When they ask you why you didn’t answer the phone, tell them you were busy.  If your family is like mine and they want you to tell them what you were doing, tell them you were having sex (that worked for me a lot) ha, ha!!</ol>
      <p class="implicit-break"></p>
        <p class="first first-in-chapter first-full-width">
        5.  Don’t answer the door unless you have to.
      </ol>
      <p class="subsq">I’ve told plenty of solicitors, “No Thank You,” without answering my door - and this is something I still do even when I’m not writing!  If you’re still ‘needed’ let everyone know you don’t answer the phone or the door after a specific time.  My time is 10 p.m.</p>
    </div>
  </div>
</body>
</html>
```

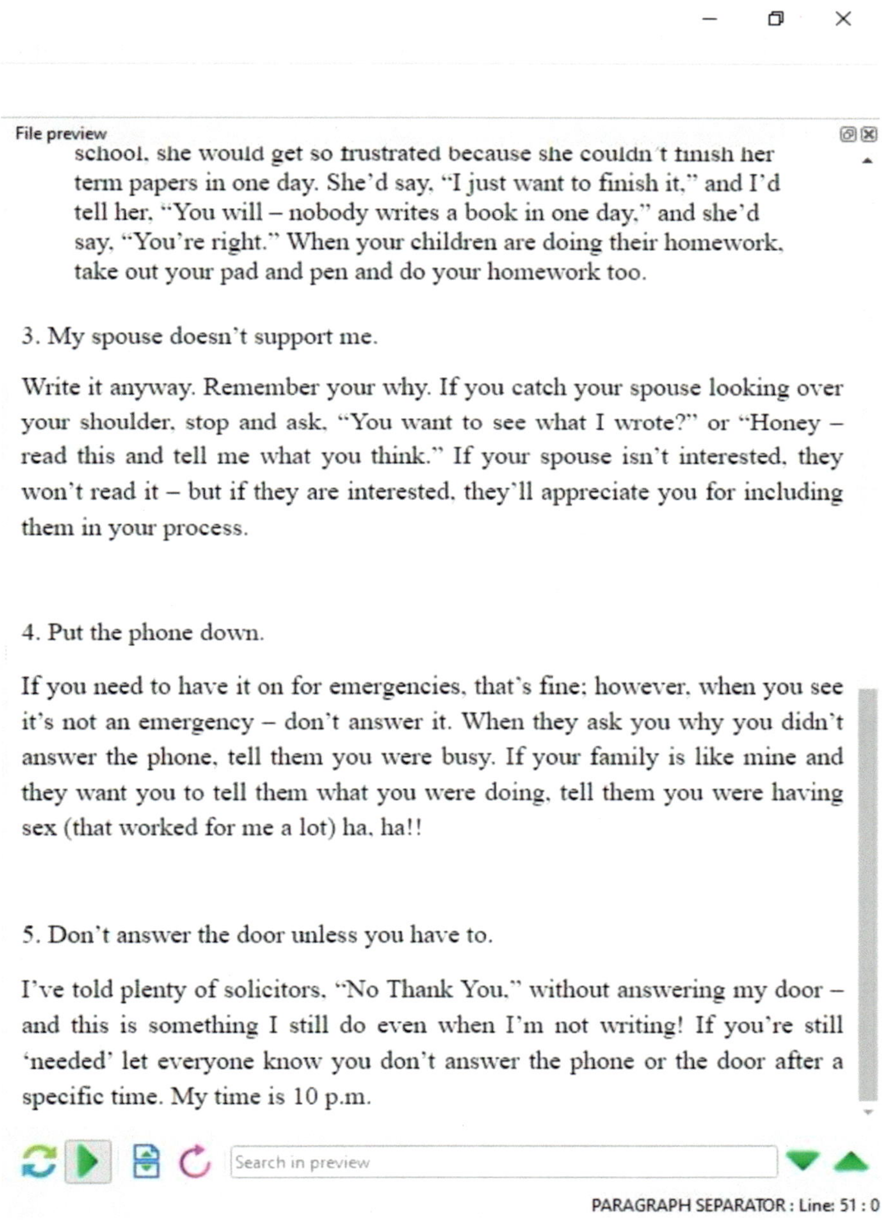

school, she would get so frustrated because she couldn't finish her term papers in one day. She'd say, "I just want to finish it," and I'd tell her, "You will – nobody writes a book in one day," and she'd say, "You're right." When your children are doing their homework, take out your pad and pen and do your homework too.

3. My spouse doesn't support me.

Write it anyway. Remember your why. If you catch your spouse looking over your shoulder, stop and ask, "You want to see what I wrote?" or "Honey – read this and tell me what you think." If your spouse isn't interested, they won't read it – but if they are interested, they'll appreciate you for including them in your process.

4. Put the phone down.

If you need to have it on for emergencies, that's fine; however, when you see it's not an emergency – don't answer it. When they ask you why you didn't answer the phone, tell them you were busy. If your family is like mine and they want you to tell them what you were doing, tell them you were having sex (that worked for me a lot) ha, ha!!

5. Don't answer the door unless you have to.

I've told plenty of solicitors, "No Thank You," without answering my door – and this is something I still do even when I'm not writing! If you're still 'needed' let everyone know you don't answer the phone or the door after a specific time. My time is 10 p.m.

When I got to 'I Wrote My Book' I saw the following:

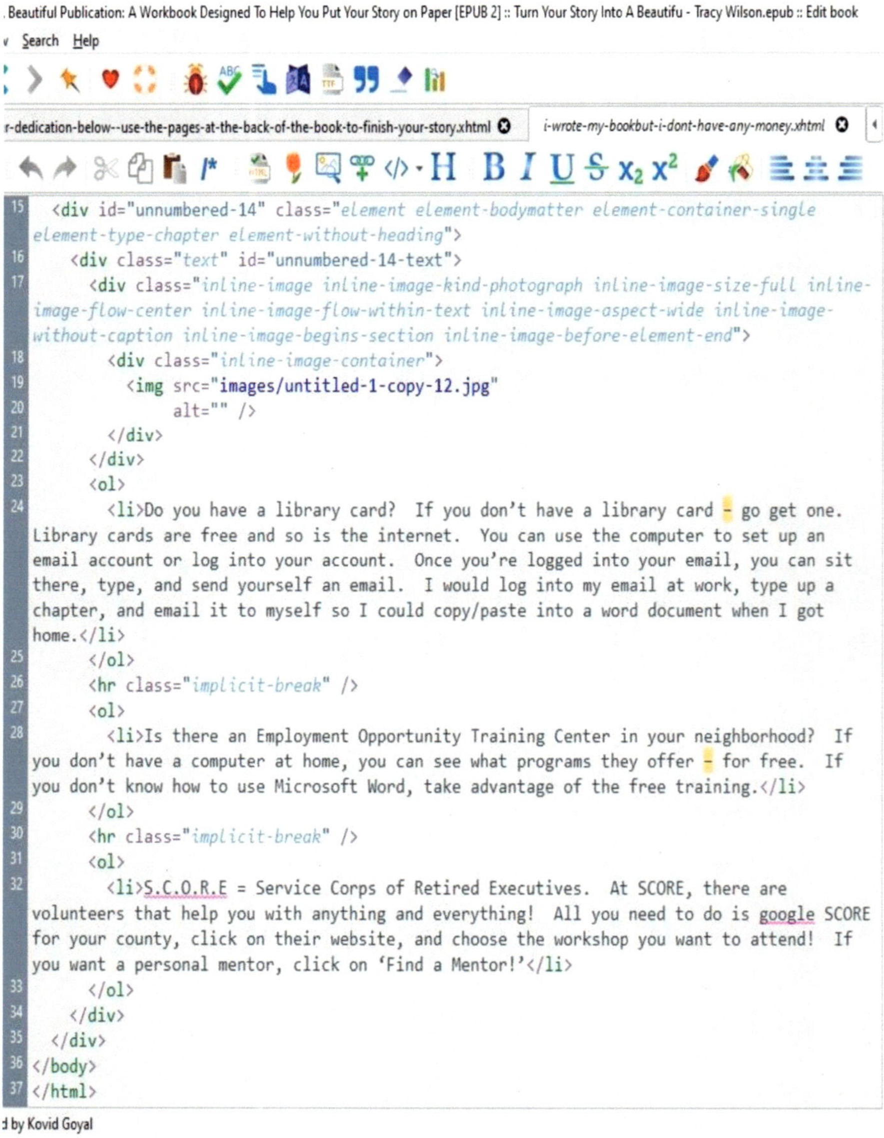


```
  <div id="unnumbered-14" class="element element-bodymatter element-container-single
element-type-chapter element-without-heading">
    <div class="text" id="unnumbered-14-text">
      <div class="inline-image inline-image-kind-photograph inline-image-size-full inline-
image-flow-center inline-image-flow-within-text inline-image-aspect-wide inline-image-
without-caption inline-image-begins-section inline-image-before-element-end">
        <div class="inline-image-container">
          <img src="images/untitled-1-copy-12.jpg"
               alt="" />
        </div>
      </div>
      <ol>
        <li>Do you have a library card?  If you don't have a library card - go get one.
Library cards are free and so is the internet.  You can use the computer to set up an
email account or log into your account.  Once you're logged into your email, you can sit
there, type, and send yourself an email.  I would log into my email at work, type up a
chapter, and email it to myself so I could copy/paste into a word document when I got
home.</li>
      </ol>
      <hr class="implicit-break" />
      <ol>
        <li>Is there an Employment Opportunity Training Center in your neighborhood?  If
you don't have a computer at home, you can see what programs they offer - for free.  If
you don't know how to use Microsoft Word, take advantage of the free training.</li>
      </ol>
      <hr class="implicit-break" />
      <ol>
        <li>S.C.O.R.E = Service Corps of Retired Executives.  At SCORE, there are
volunteers that help you with anything and everything!  All you need to do is google SCORE
for your county, click on their website, and choose the workshop you want to attend!  If
you want a personal mentor, click on 'Find a Mentor!'</li>
      </ol>
    </div>
  </div>
</body>
</html>
```

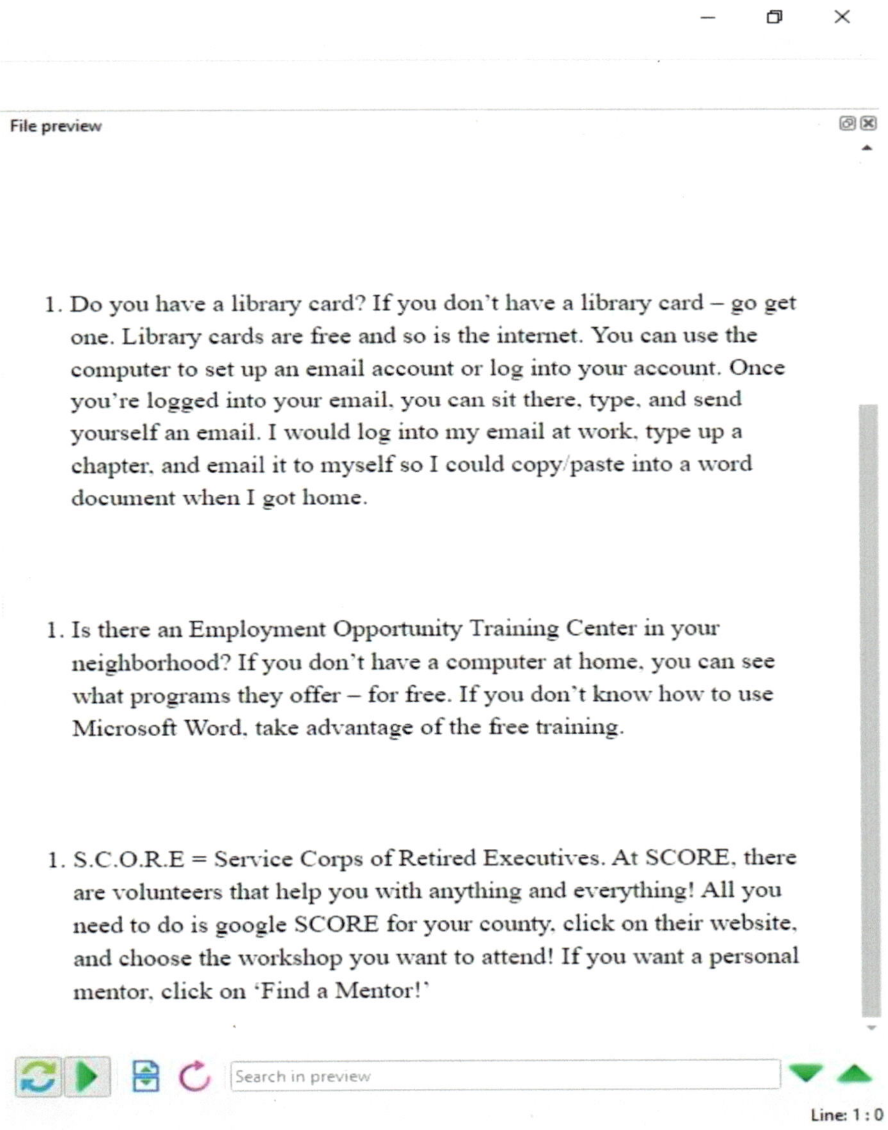

1. Do you have a library card? If you don't have a library card – go get one. Library cards are free and so is the internet. You can use the computer to set up an email account or log into your account. Once you're logged into your email, you can sit there, type, and send yourself an email. I would log into my email at work, type up a chapter, and email it to myself so I could copy/paste into a word document when I got home.

1. Is there an Employment Opportunity Training Center in your neighborhood? If you don't have a computer at home, you can see what programs they offer – for free. If you don't know how to use Microsoft Word, take advantage of the free training.

1. S.C.O.R.E = Service Corps of Retired Executives. At SCORE, there are volunteers that help you with anything and everything! All you need to do is google SCORE for your county, click on their website, and choose the workshop you want to attend! If you want a personal mentor, click on 'Find a Mentor!'

This took some time to correct because I wanted the paragraphs numbered 1, 2, 3 and I also wanted to keep them indented, so I went to google and after a few tries, I did the following:

1. I removed <hr class="implicit-break" /> between each paragraph. This made it line up better.

2. I changed <ol> at the beginning of each paragraph to <ol start="1"><li>, <ol start="2"><li>, and <ol start="3"><li>.

3. I removed </li> from the end of each paragraph.

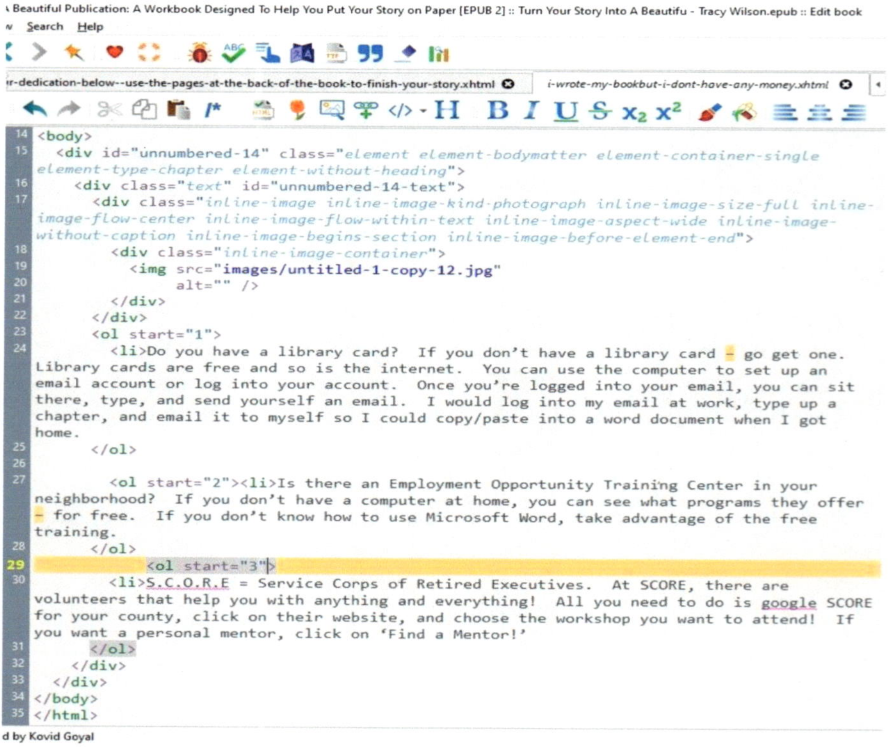

File preview

MONEY!"

1. Do you have a library card? If you don't have a library card – go get one. Library cards are free and so is the internet. You can use the computer to set up an email account or log into your account. Once you're logged into your email, you can sit there, type, and send yourself an email. I would log into my email at work, type up a chapter, and email it to myself so I could copy/paste into a word document when I got home.

2. Is there an Employment Opportunity Training Center in your neighborhood? If you don't have a computer at home, you can see what programs they offer – for free. If you don't know how to use Microsoft Word, take advantage of the free training.

3. S.C.O.R.E = Service Corps of Retired Executives. At SCORE, there are volunteers that help you with anything and everything! All you need to do is google SCORE for your county, click on their website, and choose the workshop you want to attend! If you want a personal mentor, click on 'Find a Mentor!'

Search in preview

QUOTATION MARK : Line: 29 : 25

When I got to 'I Have A Computer At Home' I saw the following:

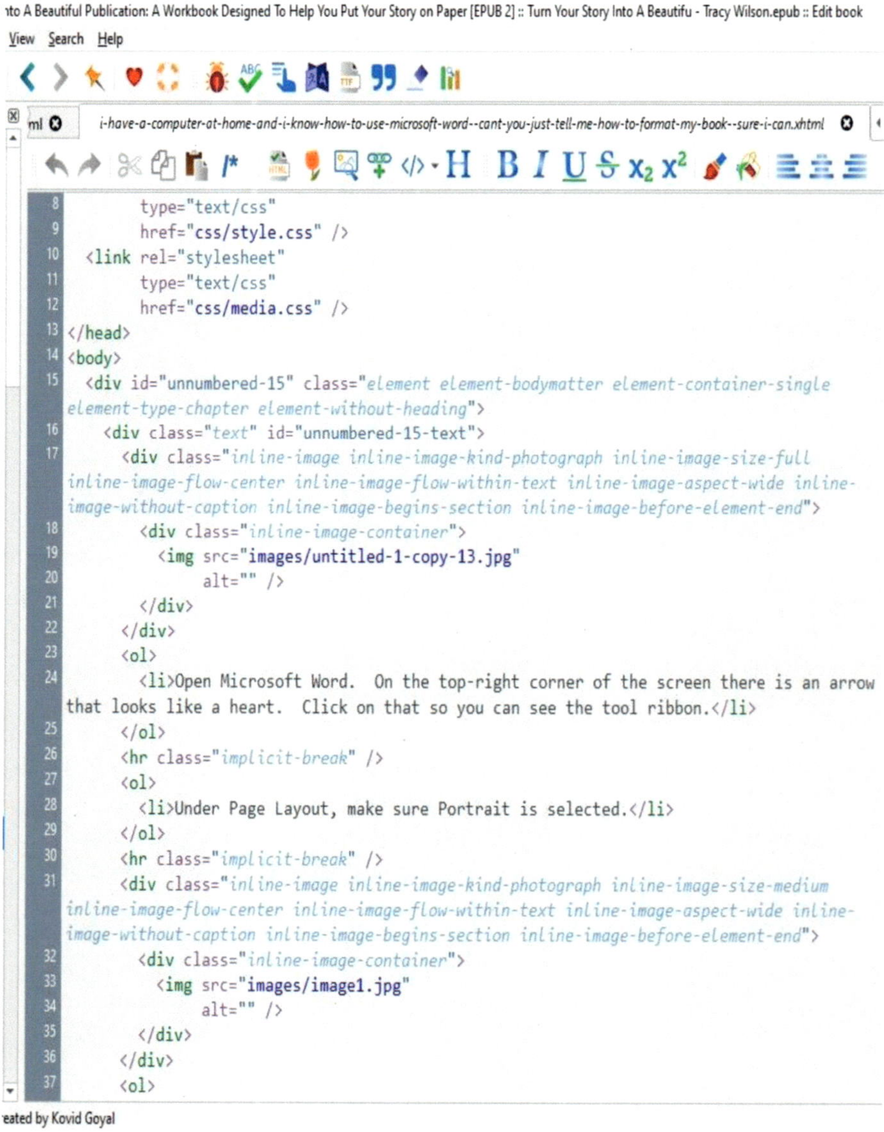

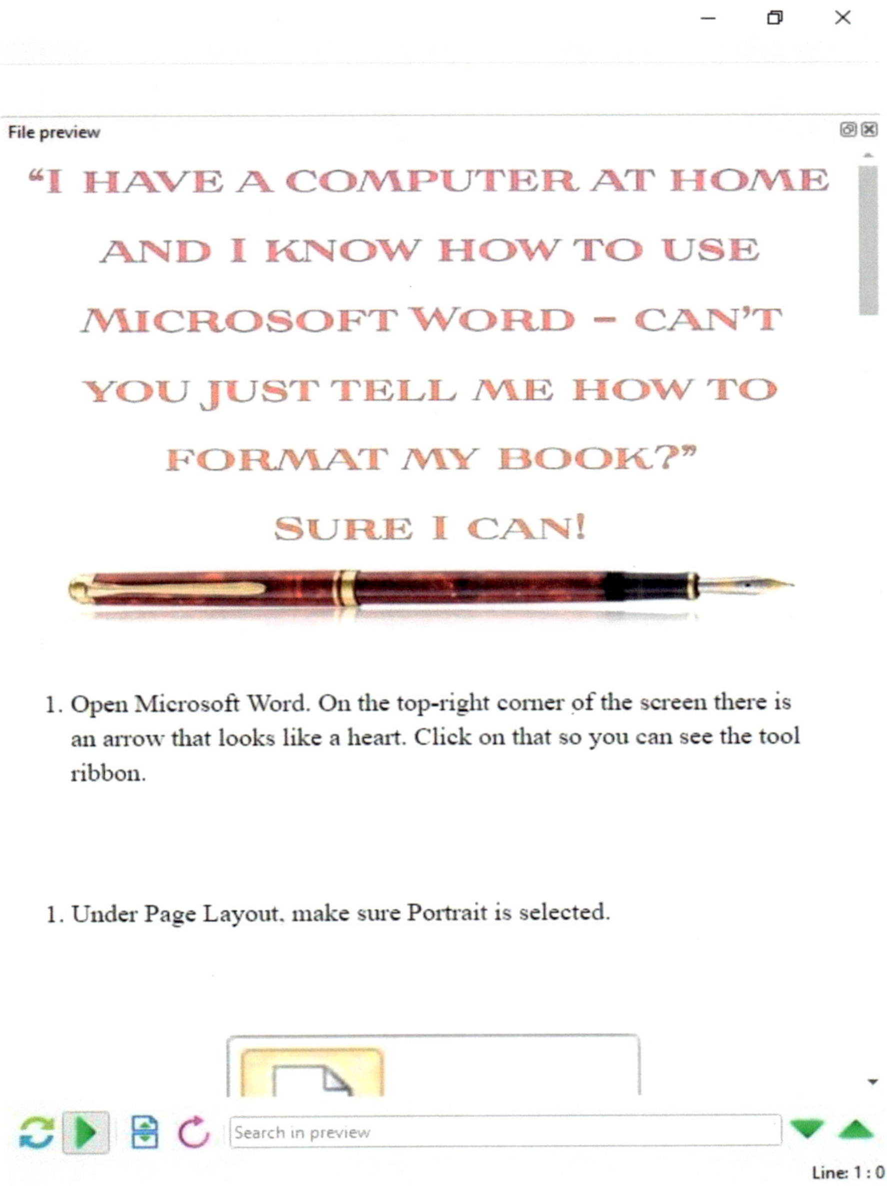
File preview
"I HAVE A COMPUTER AT HOME AND I KNOW HOW TO USE MICROSOFT WORD – CAN'T YOU JUST TELL ME HOW TO FORMAT MY BOOK?"
SURE I CAN!
1. Open Microsoft Word. On the top-right corner of the screen there is an arrow that looks like a heart. Click on that so you can see the tool ribbon.
1. Under Page Layout, make sure Portrait is selected.
Search in preview
Line: 1 : 0

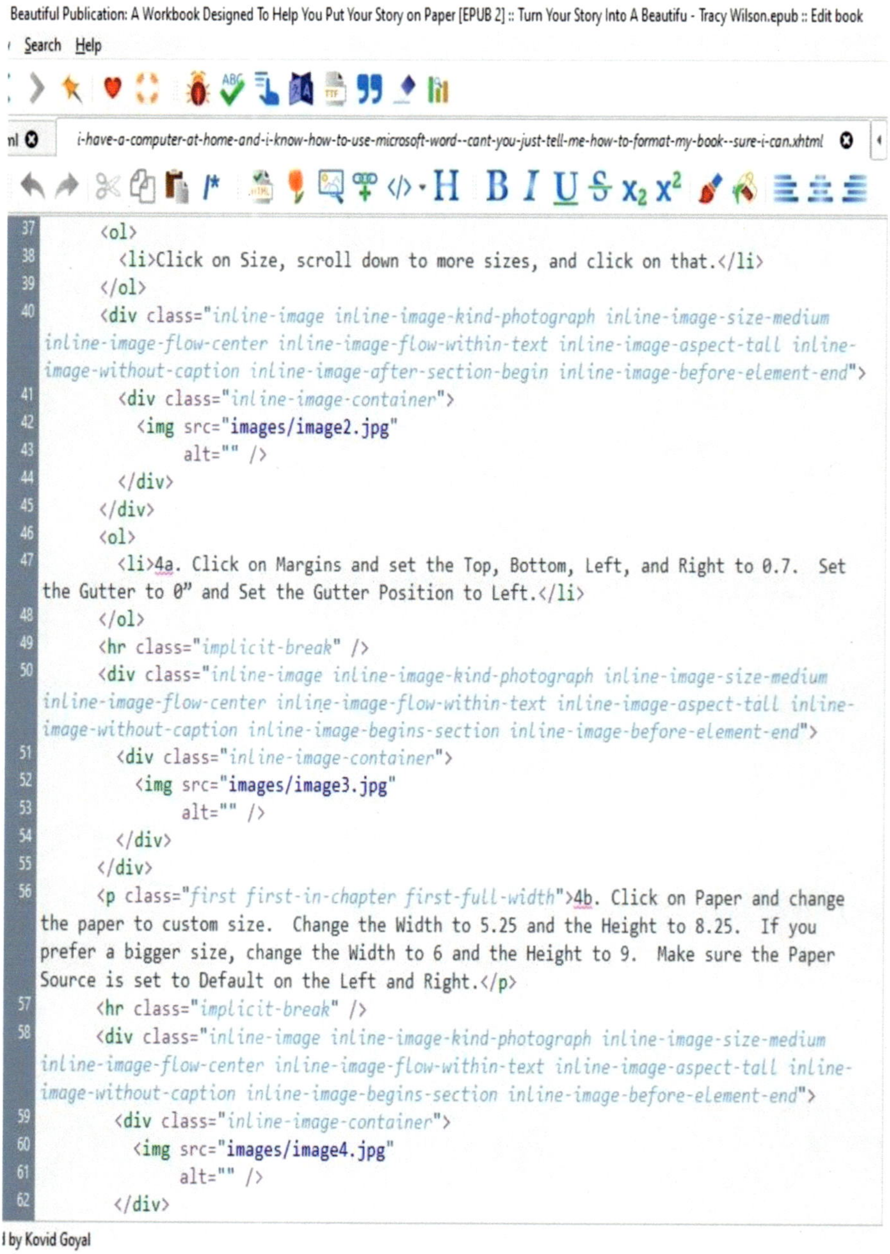


```
      <ol>
        <li>Click on Size, scroll down to more sizes, and click on that.</li>
      </ol>
      <div class="inline-image inline-image-kind-photograph inline-image-size-medium inline-image-flow-center inline-image-flow-within-text inline-image-aspect-tall inline-image-without-caption inline-image-after-section-begin inline-image-before-element-end">
        <div class="inline-image-container">
          <img src="images/image2.jpg"
               alt="" />
        </div>
      </div>
      <ol>
        <li>4a. Click on Margins and set the Top, Bottom, Left, and Right to 0.7.  Set the Gutter to 0" and Set the Gutter Position to Left.</li>
      </ol>
      <hr class="implicit-break" />
      <div class="inline-image inline-image-kind-photograph inline-image-size-medium inline-image-flow-center inline-image-flow-within-text inline-image-aspect-tall inline-image-without-caption inline-image-begins-section inline-image-before-element-end">
        <div class="inline-image-container">
          <img src="images/image3.jpg"
               alt="" />
        </div>
      </div>
      <p class="first first-in-chapter first-full-width">4b. Click on Paper and change the paper to custom size.  Change the Width to 5.25 and the Height to 8.25.  If you prefer a bigger size, change the Width to 6 and the Height to 9.  Make sure the Paper Source is set to Default on the Left and Right.</p>
      <hr class="implicit-break" />
      <div class="inline-image inline-image-kind-photograph inline-image-size-medium inline-image-flow-center inline-image-flow-within-text inline-image-aspect-tall inline-image-without-caption inline-image-begins-section inline-image-before-element-end">
        <div class="inline-image-container">
          <img src="images/image4.jpg"
               alt="" />
        </div>
```

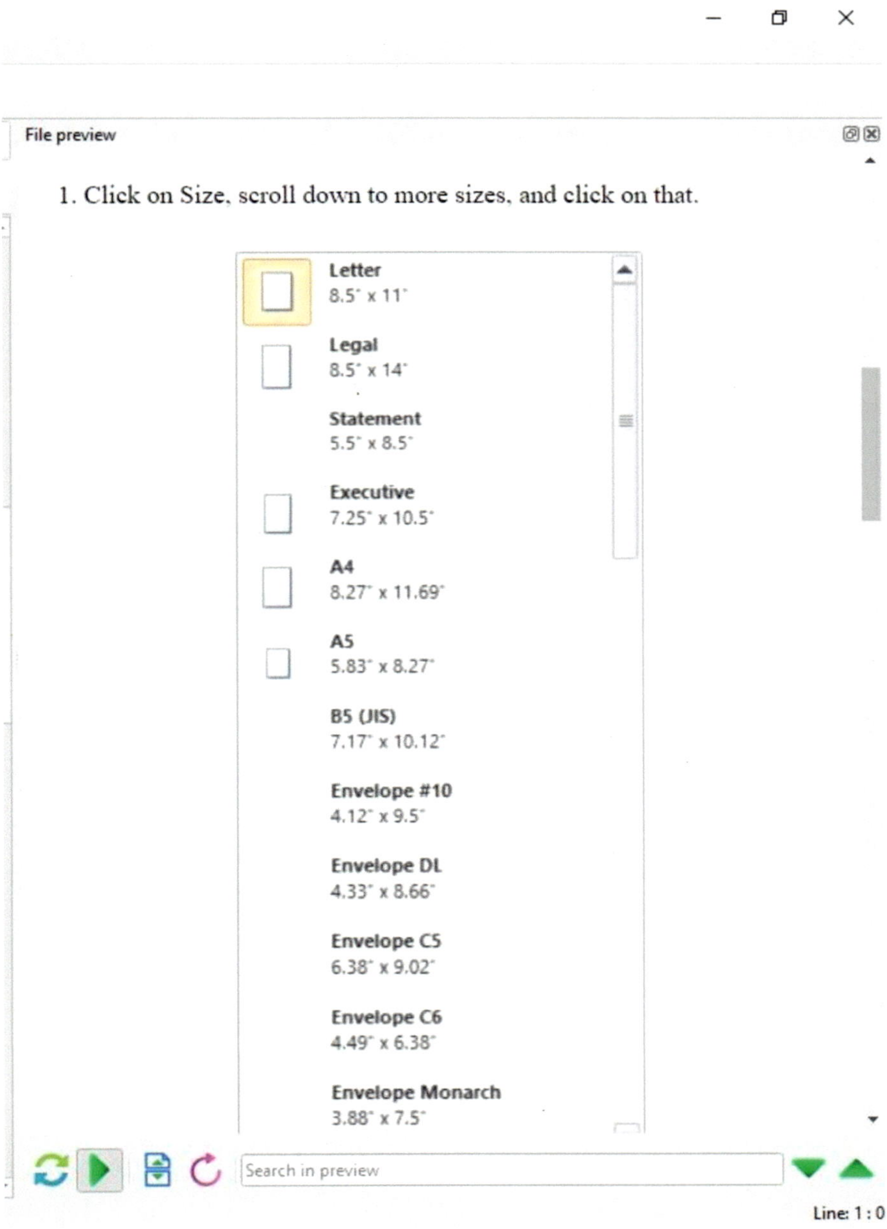
File preview
1. Click on Size, scroll down to more sizes, and click on that.
Letter
8.5" x 11"
Legal
8.5" x 14"
Statement
5.5" x 8.5"
Executive
7.25" x 10.5"
A4
8.27" x 11.69"
A5
5.83" x 8.27"
B5 (JIS)
7.17" x 10.12"
Envelope #10
4.12" x 9.5"
Envelope DL
4.33" x 8.66"
Envelope C5
6.38" x 9.02"
Envelope C6
4.49" x 6.38"
Envelope Monarch
3.88" x 7.5"
Search in preview
Line: 1 : 0

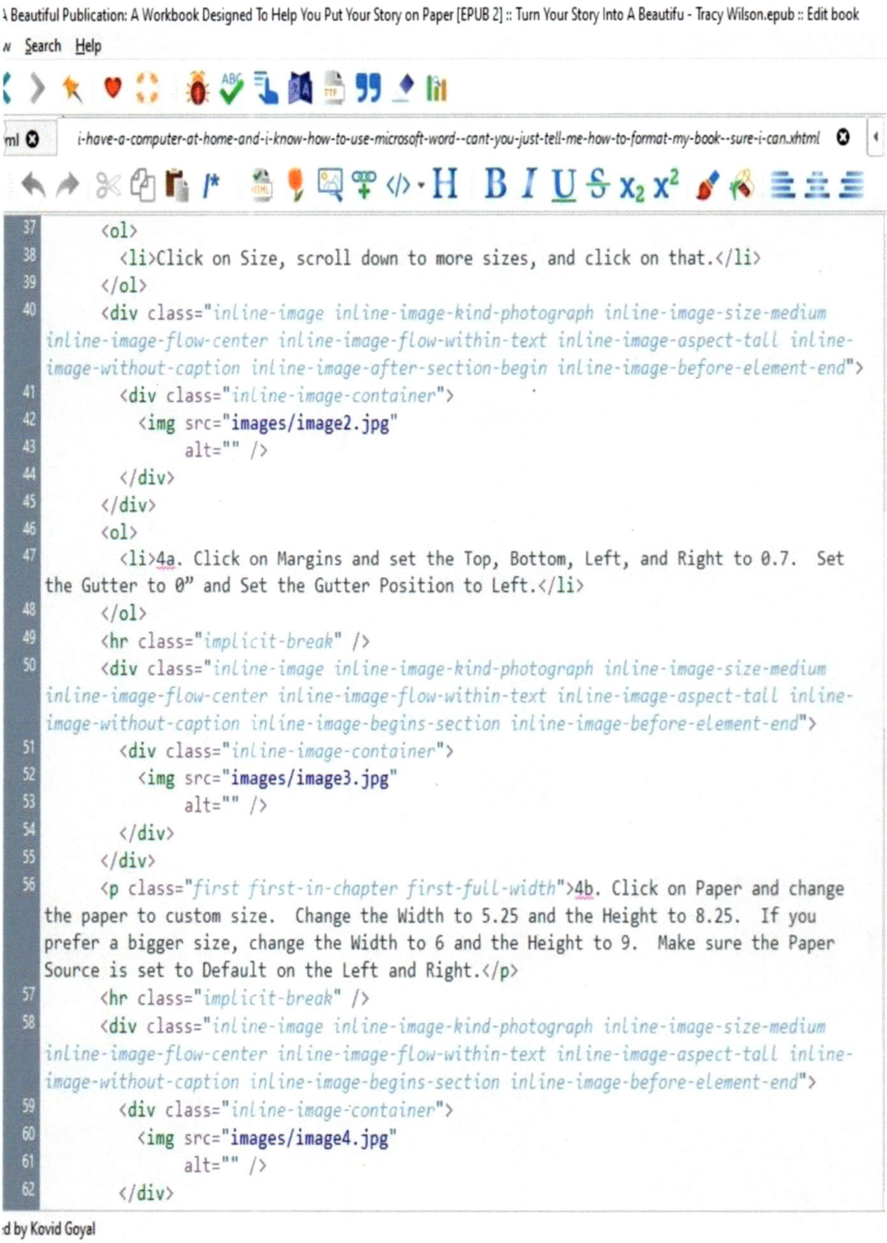


```
      <ol>
        <li>Click on Size, scroll down to more sizes, and click on that.</li>
      </ol>
      <div class="inline-image inline-image-kind-photograph inline-image-size-medium inline-image-flow-center inline-image-flow-within-text inline-image-aspect-tall inline-image-without-caption inline-image-after-section-begin inline-image-before-element-end">
        <div class="inline-image-container">
          <img src="images/image2.jpg"
               alt="" />
        </div>
      </div>
      <ol>
        <li>4a. Click on Margins and set the Top, Bottom, Left, and Right to 0.7.  Set the Gutter to 0” and Set the Gutter Position to Left.</li>
      </ol>
      <hr class="implicit-break" />
      <div class="inline-image inline-image-kind-photograph inline-image-size-medium inline-image-flow-center inline-image-flow-within-text inline-image-aspect-tall inline-image-without-caption inline-image-begins-section inline-image-before-element-end">
        <div class="inline-image-container">
          <img src="images/image3.jpg"
               alt="" />
        </div>
      </div>
      <p class="first first-in-chapter first-full-width">4b. Click on Paper and change the paper to custom size.  Change the Width to 5.25 and the Height to 8.25.  If you prefer a bigger size, change the Width to 6 and the Height to 9.  Make sure the Paper Source is set to Default on the Left and Right.</p>
      <hr class="implicit-break" />
      <div class="inline-image inline-image-kind-photograph inline-image-size-medium inline-image-flow-center inline-image-flow-within-text inline-image-aspect-tall inline-image-without-caption inline-image-begins-section inline-image-before-element-end">
        <div class="inline-image-container">
          <img src="images/image4.jpg"
               alt="" />
        </div>
```

File preview

1. 4a. Click on Margins and set the Top, Bottom, Left, and Right to 0.7. Set the Gutter to 0" and Set the Gutter Position to Left.

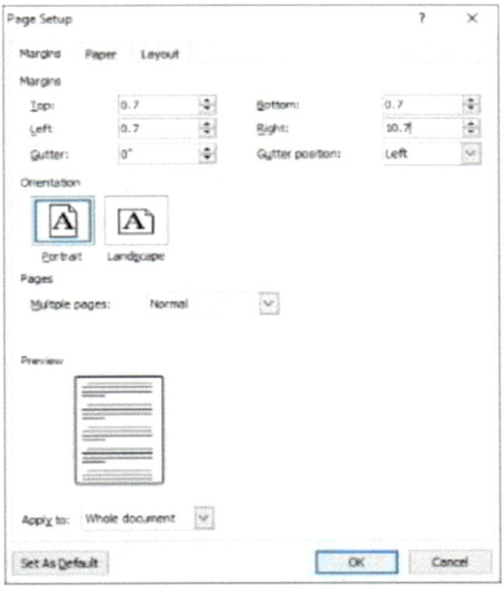

4b. Click on Paper and change the paper to custom size. Change the Width to 5.25 and the Height to 8.25. If you prefer a bigger size, change the Width to 6 and the Height to 9. Make sure the Paper Source is set to Default on the Left and Right.

Search in preview

Line: 1 : 0

This was easier to correct because of all the steps I took previously:

1. I changed <ol> at the beginning of each paragraph to <ol start="1"><li>, <ol start="2"><li>, and <ol start="3"><li>.

2. I removed <p class="first first-in-chapter first-full-width"> from in front of 4b. and replaced it with <ol>, but I left it in front of 4c. through 4h.

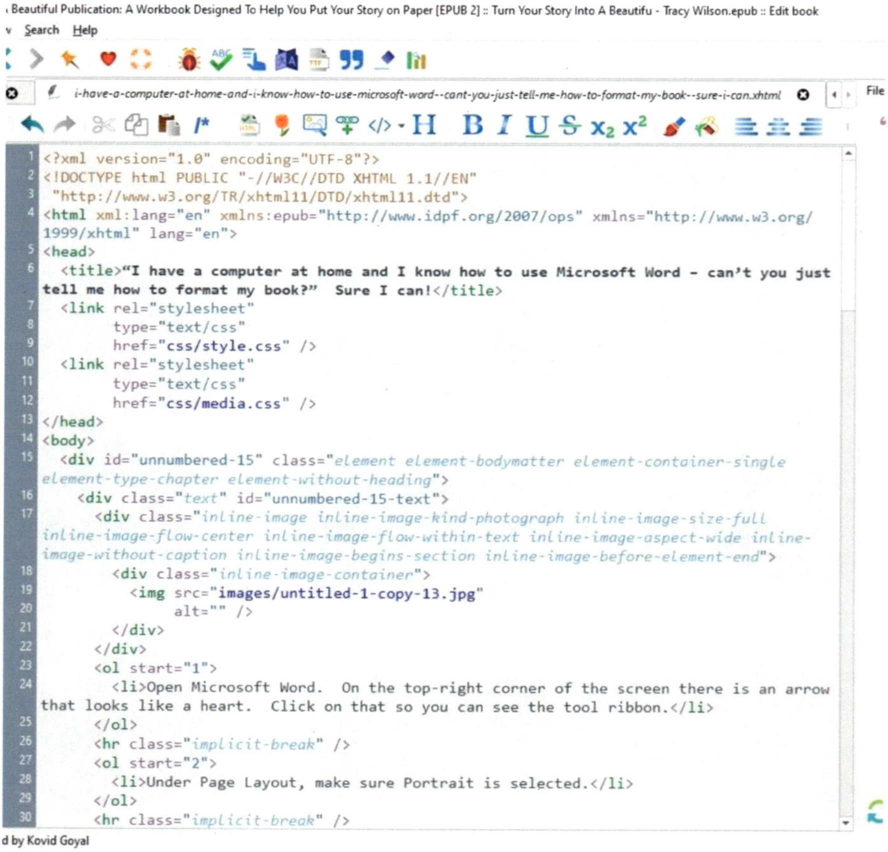


```
<?xml version="1.0" encoding="UTF-8"?>
<!DOCTYPE html PUBLIC "-//W3C//DTD XHTML 1.1//EN"
 "http://www.w3.org/TR/xhtml11/DTD/xhtml11.dtd">
<html xml:lang="en" xmlns:epub="http://www.idpf.org/2007/ops" xmlns="http://www.w3.org/1999/xhtml" lang="en">
<head>
  <title>“I have a computer at home and I know how to use Microsoft Word - can’t you just tell me how to format my book?”  Sure I can!</title>
  <link rel="stylesheet"
        type="text/css"
        href="css/style.css" />
  <link rel="stylesheet"
        type="text/css"
        href="css/media.css" />
</head>
<body>
  <div id="unnumbered-15" class="element element-bodymatter element-container-single element-type-chapter element-without-heading">
    <div class="text" id="unnumbered-15-text">
      <div class="inline-image inline-image-kind-photograph inline-image-size-full inline-image-flow-center inline-image-flow-within-text inline-image-aspect-wide inline-image-without-caption inline-image-begins-section inline-image-before-element-end">
        <div class="inline-image-container">
          <img src="images/untitled-1-copy-13.jpg"
               alt="" />
        </div>
      </div>
      <ol start="1">
        <li>Open Microsoft Word.  On the top-right corner of the screen there is an arrow that looks like a heart.  Click on that so you can see the tool ribbon.</li>
      </ol>
      <hr class="implicit-break" />
      <ol start="2">
        <li>Under Page Layout, make sure Portrait is selected.</li>
      </ol>
      <hr class="implicit-break" />
```

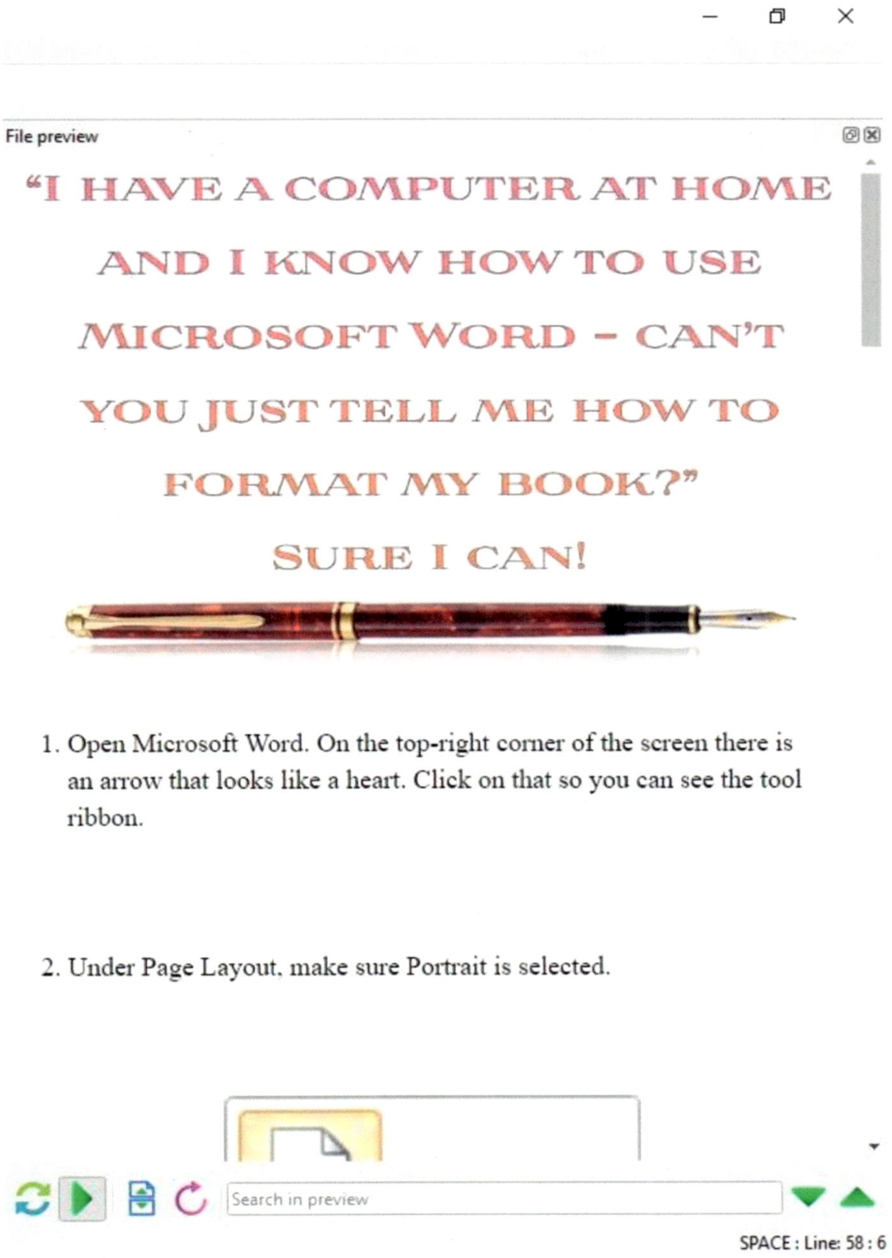
File preview
"I HAVE A COMPUTER AT HOME AND I KNOW HOW TO USE MICROSOFT WORD - CAN'T YOU JUST TELL ME HOW TO FORMAT MY BOOK?"
SURE I CAN!
1. Open Microsoft Word. On the top-right corner of the screen there is an arrow that looks like a heart. Click on that so you can see the tool ribbon.
2. Under Page Layout, make sure Portrait is selected.
Search in preview
SPACE : Line: 58 : 6

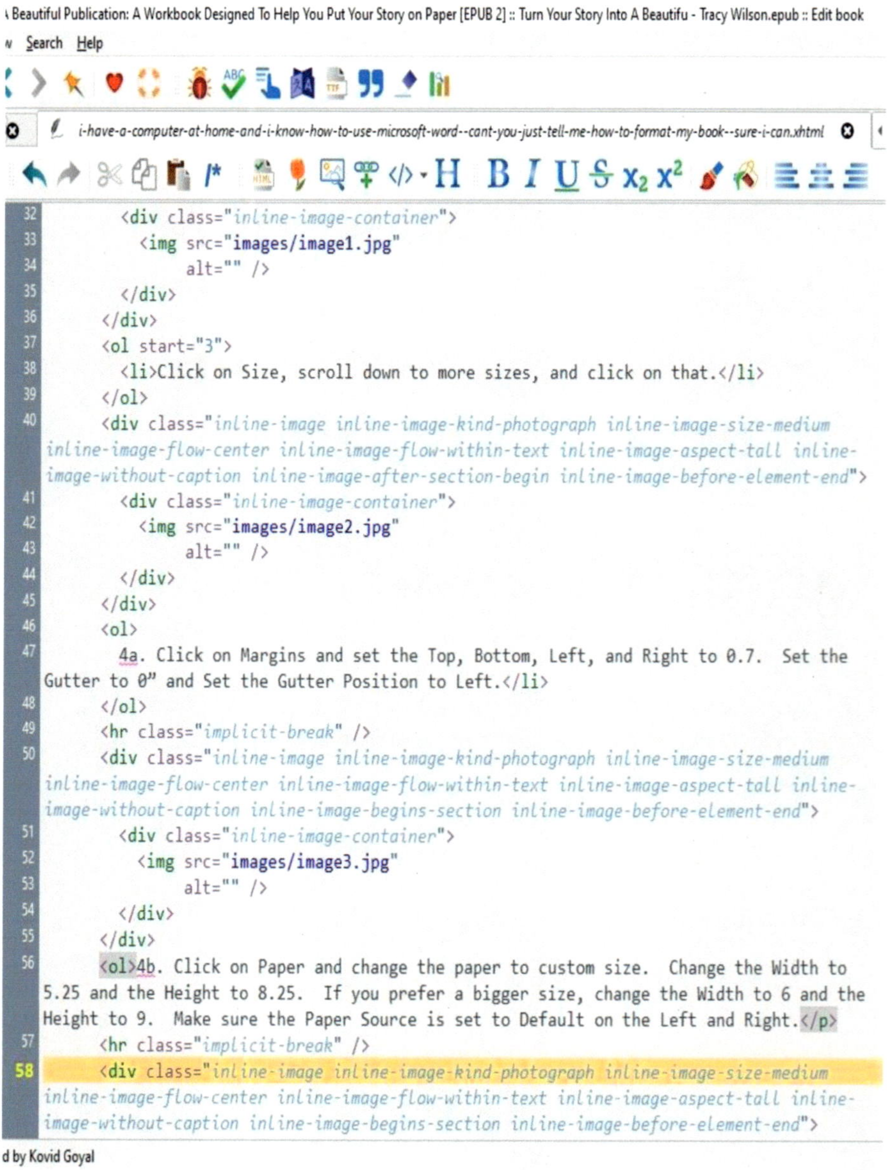


```
        <div class="inline-image-container">
          <img src="images/image1.jpg"
               alt="" />
        </div>
      </div>
      <ol start="3">
        <li>Click on Size, scroll down to more sizes, and click on that.</li>
      </ol>
      <div class="inline-image inline-image-kind-photograph inline-image-size-medium inline-image-flow-center inline-image-flow-within-text inline-image-aspect-tall inline-image-without-caption inline-image-after-section-begin inline-image-before-element-end">
        <div class="inline-image-container">
          <img src="images/image2.jpg"
               alt="" />
        </div>
      </div>
      <ol>
        4a. Click on Margins and set the Top, Bottom, Left, and Right to 0.7.  Set the Gutter to 0” and Set the Gutter Position to Left.</li>
      </ol>
      <hr class="implicit-break" />
      <div class="inline-image inline-image-kind-photograph inline-image-size-medium inline-image-flow-center inline-image-flow-within-text inline-image-aspect-tall inline-image-without-caption inline-image-begins-section inline-image-before-element-end">
        <div class="inline-image-container">
          <img src="images/image3.jpg"
               alt="" />
        </div>
      </div>
      <ol>4b. Click on Paper and change the paper to custom size.  Change the Width to 5.25 and the Height to 8.25.  If you prefer a bigger size, change the Width to 6 and the Height to 9.  Make sure the Paper Source is set to Default on the Left and Right.</p>
      <hr class="implicit-break" />
      <div class="inline-image inline-image-kind-photograph inline-image-size-medium inline-image-flow-center inline-image-flow-within-text inline-image-aspect-tall inline-image-without-caption inline-image-begins-section inline-image-before-element-end">
```

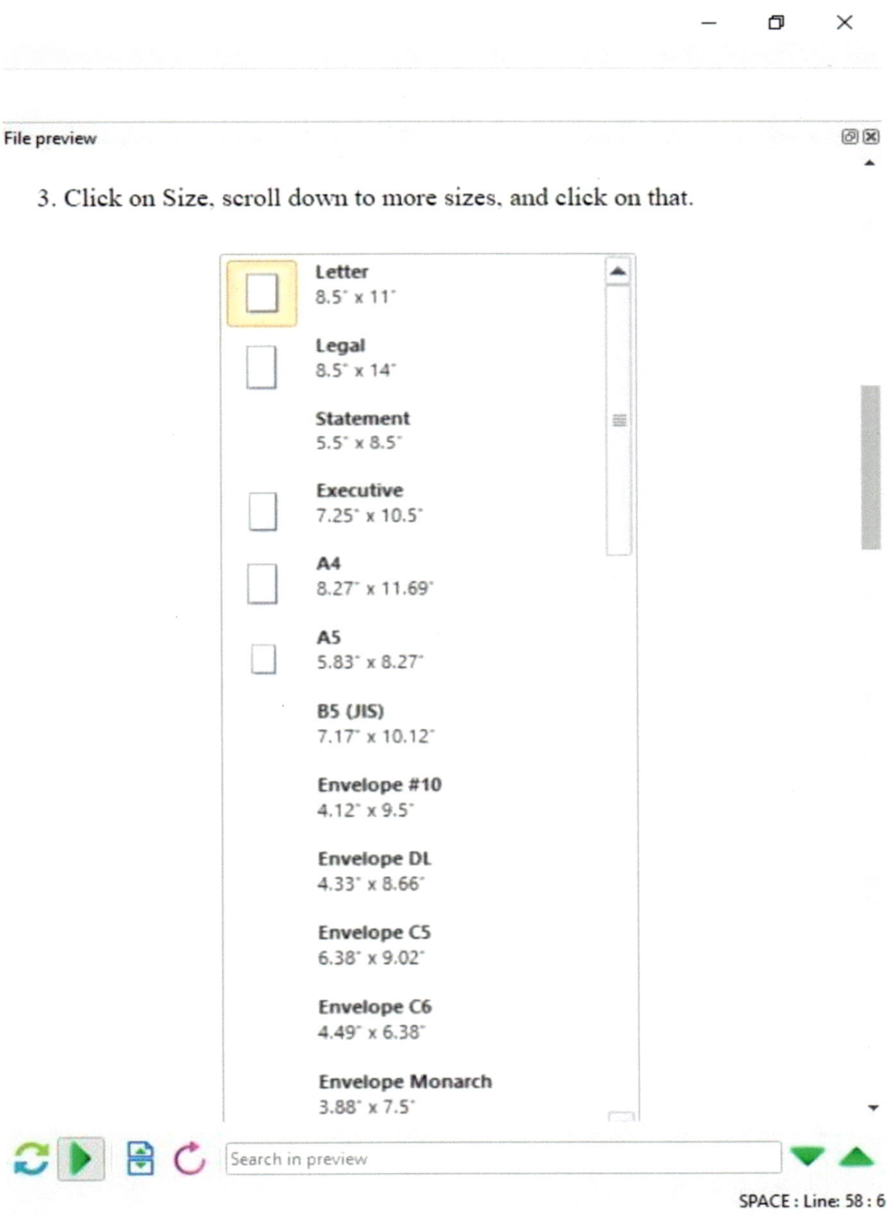
File preview
3. Click on Size, scroll down to more sizes, and click on that.
Letter
8.5" x 11"
Legal
8.5" x 14"
Statement
5.5" x 8.5"
Executive
7.25" x 10.5"
A4
8.27" x 11.69"
A5
5.83" x 8.27"
B5 (JIS)
7.17" x 10.12"
Envelope #10
4.12" x 9.5"
Envelope DL
4.33" x 8.66"
Envelope C5
6.38" x 9.02"
Envelope C6
4.49" x 6.38"
Envelope Monarch
3.88" x 7.5"
Search in preview
SPACE : Line: 58 : 6

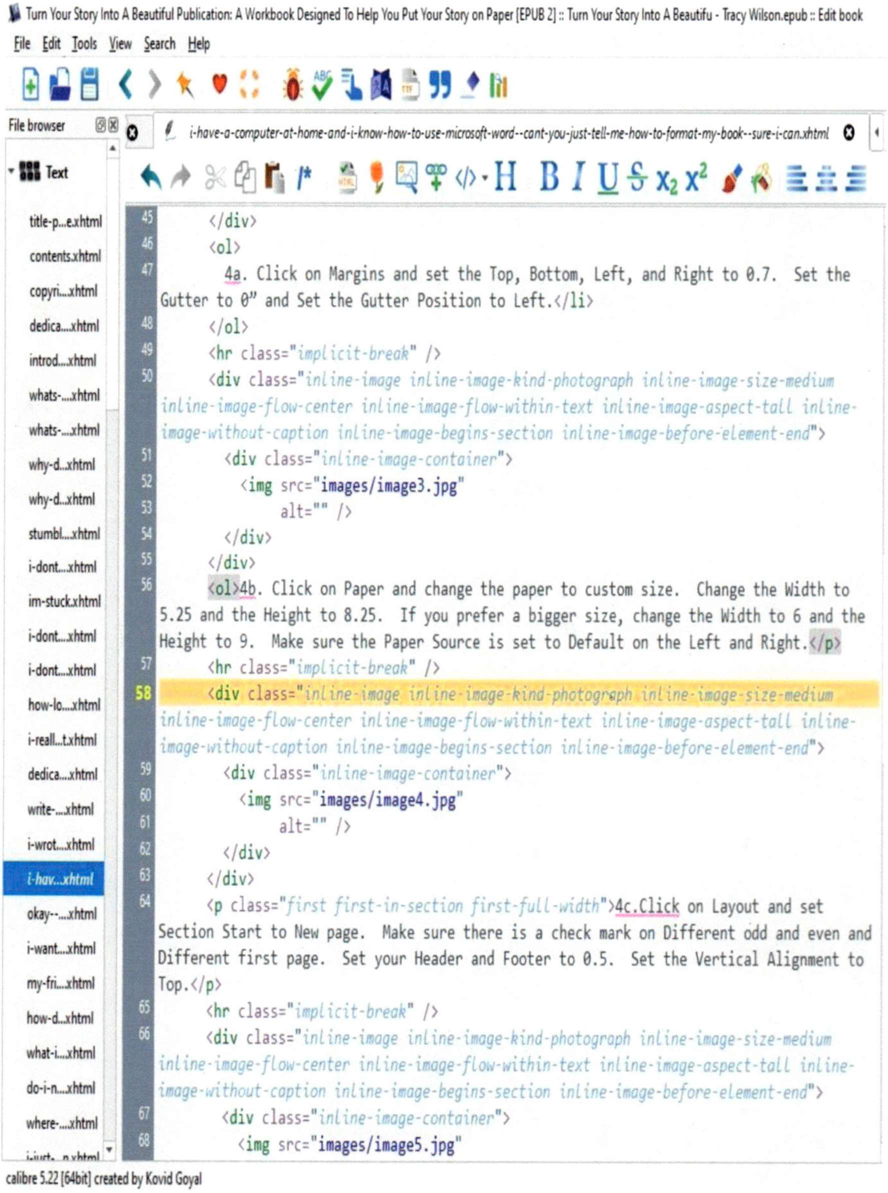
Turn Your Story Into A Beautiful Publication: A Workbook Designed To Help You Put Your Story on Paper [EPUB 2] :: Turn Your Story Into A Beautifu - Tracy Wilson.epub :: Edit book
File Edit Tools View Search Help
File browser
i-have-a-computer-at-home-and-i-know-how-to-use-microsoft-word--cant-you-just-tell-me-how-to-format-my-book--sure-i-can.xhtml
Text
title-p...e.xhtml
contents.xhtml
copyri...xhtml
dedica...xhtml
introd...xhtml
whats-...xhtml
whats-...xhtml
why-d...xhtml
why-d...xhtml
stumbl...xhtml
i-dont...xhtml
im-stuck.xhtml
i-dont...xhtml
i-dont...xhtml
how-lo...xhtml
i-reall...t.xhtml
dedica...xhtml
write-...xhtml
i-wrot...xhtml
i-hav...xhtml
okay-...xhtml
i-want...xhtml
my-fri...xhtml
how-d...xhtml
what-i...xhtml
do-i-n...xhtml
where-...xhtml
</div>
<ol>
4a. Click on Margins and set the Top, Bottom, Left, and Right to 0.7. Set the Gutter to 0" and Set the Gutter Position to Left.</li>
</ol>
<hr class="implicit-break" />
<div class="inline-image inline-image-kind-photograph inline-image-size-medium inline-image-flow-center inline-image-flow-within-text inline-image-aspect-tall inline-image-without-caption inline-image-begins-section inline-image-before-element-end">
<div class="inline-image-container">
<img src="images/image3.jpg"
alt="" />
</div>
</div>
<ol>4b. Click on Paper and change the paper to custom size. Change the Width to 5.25 and the Height to 8.25. If you prefer a bigger size, change the Width to 6 and the Height to 9. Make sure the Paper Source is set to Default on the Left and Right.</p>
<hr class="implicit-break" />
<div class="inline-image inline-image-kind-photograph inline-image-size-medium inline-image-flow-center inline-image-flow-within-text inline-image-aspect-tall inline-image-without-caption inline-image-begins-section inline-image-before-element-end">
<div class="inline-image-container">
<img src="images/image4.jpg"
alt="" />
</div>
</div>
<p class="first first-in-section first-full-width">4c.Click on Layout and set Section Start to New page. Make sure there is a check mark on Different odd and even and Different first page. Set your Header and Footer to 0.5. Set the Vertical Alignment to Top.</p>
<hr class="implicit-break" />
<div class="inline-image inline-image-kind-photograph inline-image-size-medium inline-image-flow-center inline-image-flow-within-text inline-image-aspect-tall inline-image-without-caption inline-image-begins-section inline-image-before-element-end">
<div class="inline-image-container">
<img src="images/image5.jpg"
calibre 5.22 [64bit] created by Kovid Goyal

File preview

4a. Click on Margins and set the Top, Bottom, Left, and Right to 0.7. Set the Gutter to 0" and Set the Gutter Position to Left.

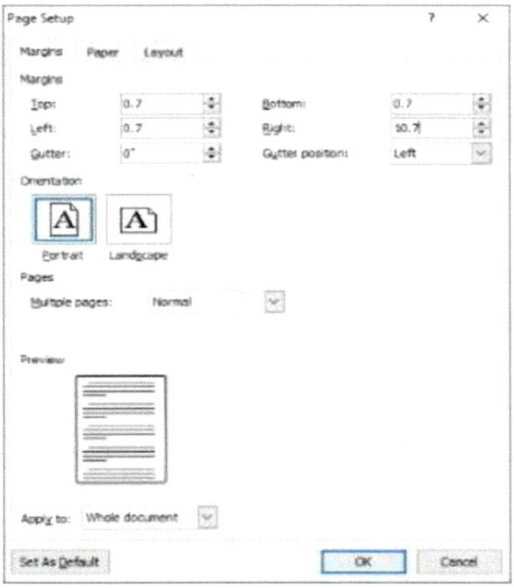

4b. Click on Paper and change the paper to custom size. Change the Width to 5.25 and the Height to 8.25. If you prefer a bigger size, change the Width to 6 and the Height to 9. Make sure the Paper Source is set to Default on the Left and Right.

Search in preview

SPACE : Line: 58 : 6

When I got to ‘Okay – I’m Ready’ I saw the following:

```
. Beautiful Publication: A Workbook Designed To Help You Put Your Story on Paper [EPUB 2] :: Turn Your Story Into A Beautifu - Tracy Wilson.epub :: Edit book
Search  Help
an.xhtml   okay--im-ready-to-upload-my-book--thats-great--once-youve-completed-these-final-steps-youll-have-everything-you-need.xhtml

<?xml version="1.0" encoding="UTF-8"?>
<!DOCTYPE html PUBLIC "-//W3C//DTD XHTML 1.1//EN"
 "http://www.w3.org/TR/xhtml11/DTD/xhtml11.dtd">
<html xml:lang="en" xmlns:epub="http://www.idpf.org/2007/ops" xmlns="http://www.w3.org/
1999/xhtml" lang="en">
<head>
  <title>“Okay - I’m ready to upload my book!”  That’s great!  Once you’ve completed these
final steps, you’ll have everything you need!</title>
  <link rel="stylesheet"
        type="text/css"
        href="css/style.css" />
  <link rel="stylesheet"
        type="text/css"
        href="css/media.css" />
</head>
<body>
  <div id="unnumbered-16" class="element element-bodymatter element-container-single
element-type-chapter element-without-heading">
    <div class="text" id="unnumbered-16-text">
      <div class="inline-image inline-image-kind-photograph inline-image-size-full inline-
image-flow-center inline-image-flow-within-text inline-image-aspect-wide inline-image-
without-caption inline-image-begins-section inline-image-before-element-end">
        <div class="inline-image-container">
          <img src="images/untitled-1-copy-14.jpg"
               alt="" />
        </div>
      </div>
      <hr class="implicit-break" />
      <ol>
        <li>Create a 2<sup>nd</sup> email account to use for your books.  Don’t use the
same email account you use for social media or shopping on Amazon.  You need to keep a
separate account for your books.</li>
      </ol>
      <hr class="implicit-break" />
      <ol>
        <li>Go to <a class="content-external-link text-is-url" href="http://
d by Kovid Goyal
```

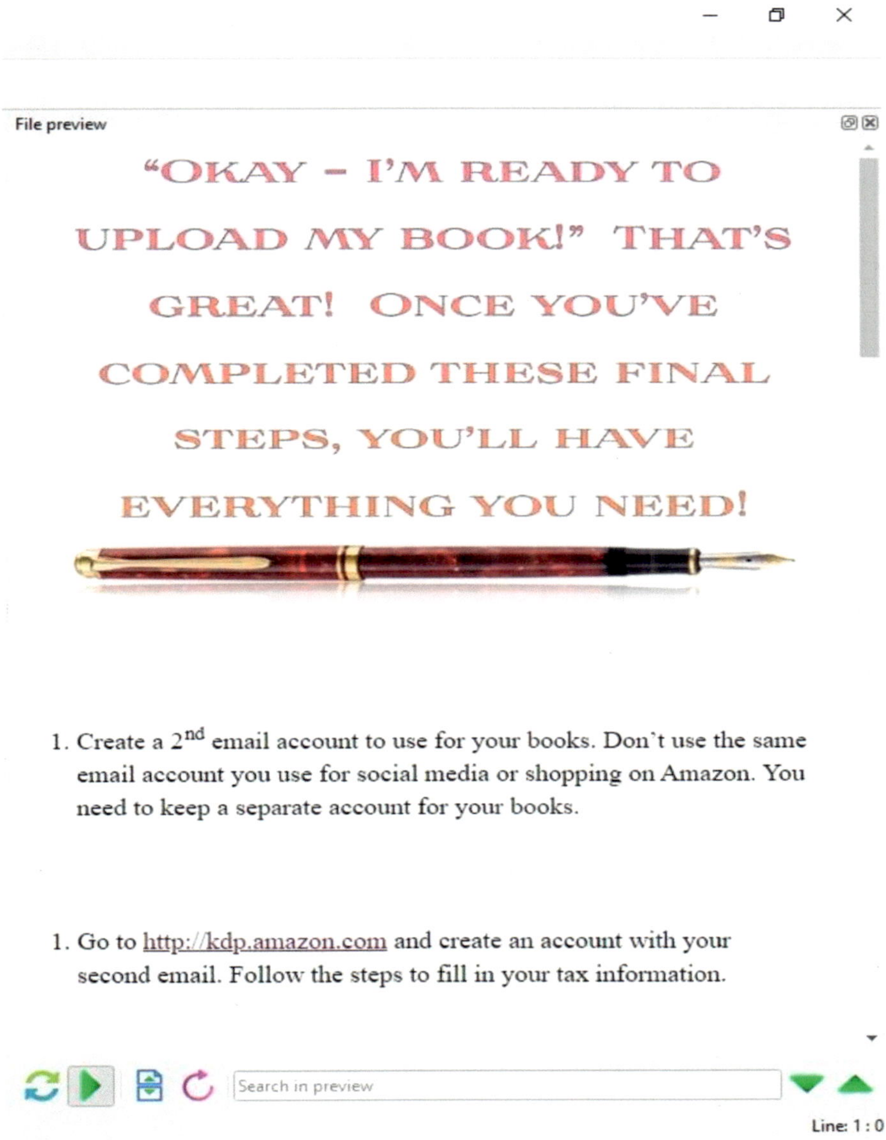

File preview

"OKAY – I'M READY TO UPLOAD MY BOOK!" THAT'S GREAT! ONCE YOU'VE COMPLETED THESE FINAL STEPS, YOU'LL HAVE EVERYTHING YOU NEED!

1. Create a 2nd email account to use for your books. Don't use the same email account you use for social media or shopping on Amazon. You need to keep a separate account for your books.

1. Go to http://kdp.amazon.com and create an account with your second email. Follow the steps to fill in your tax information.

Search in preview

Line: 1 : 0

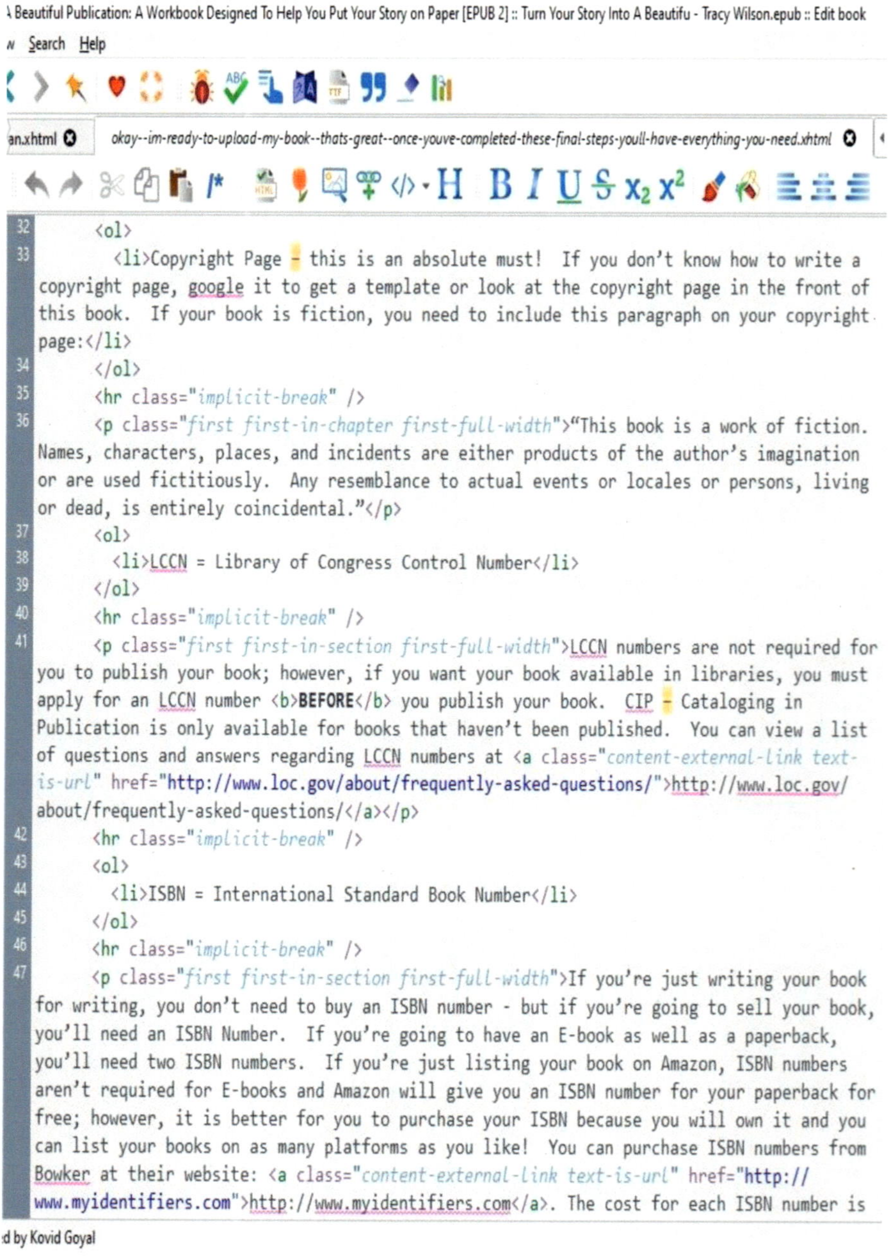


```
<ol>
  <li>Copyright Page - this is an absolute must!  If you don't know how to write a copyright page, google it to get a template or look at the copyright page in the front of this book.  If your book is fiction, you need to include this paragraph on your copyright page:</li>
</ol>
<hr class="implicit-break" />
<p class="first first-in-chapter first-full-width">"This book is a work of fiction. Names, characters, places, and incidents are either products of the author's imagination or are used fictitiously.  Any resemblance to actual events or locales or persons, living or dead, is entirely coincidental."</p>
<ol>
  <li>LCCN = Library of Congress Control Number</li>
</ol>
<hr class="implicit-break" />
<p class="first first-in-section first-full-width">LCCN numbers are not required for you to publish your book; however, if you want your book available in libraries, you must apply for an LCCN number <b>BEFORE</b> you publish your book.  CIP - Cataloging in Publication is only available for books that haven't been published.  You can view a list of questions and answers regarding LCCN numbers at <a class="content-external-link text-is-url" href="http://www.loc.gov/about/frequently-asked-questions/">http://www.loc.gov/about/frequently-asked-questions/</a></p>
<hr class="implicit-break" />
<ol>
  <li>ISBN = International Standard Book Number</li>
</ol>
<hr class="implicit-break" />
<p class="first first-in-section first-full-width">If you're just writing your book for writing, you don't need to buy an ISBN number - but if you're going to sell your book, you'll need an ISBN Number.  If you're going to have an E-book as well as a paperback, you'll need two ISBN numbers.  If you're just listing your book on Amazon, ISBN numbers aren't required for E-books and Amazon will give you an ISBN number for your paperback for free; however, it is better for you to purchase your ISBN because you will own it and you can list your books on as many platforms as you like!  You can purchase ISBN numbers from Bowker at their website: <a class="content-external-link text-is-url" href="http://www.myidentifiers.com">http://www.myidentifiers.com</a>. The cost for each ISBN number is
```

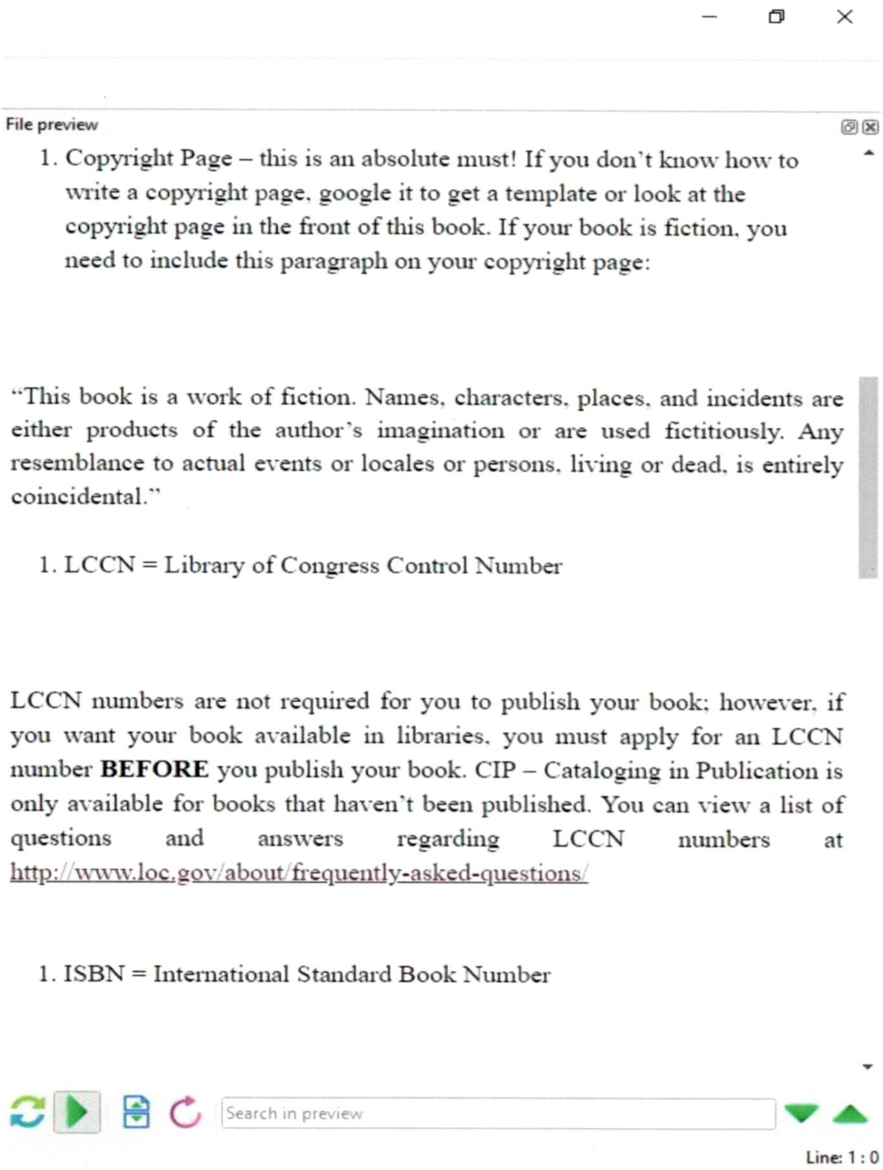

1. Copyright Page – this is an absolute must! If you don't know how to write a copyright page, google it to get a template or look at the copyright page in the front of this book. If your book is fiction, you need to include this paragraph on your copyright page:

"This book is a work of fiction. Names, characters, places, and incidents are either products of the author's imagination or are used fictitiously. Any resemblance to actual events or locales or persons, living or dead, is entirely coincidental."

1. LCCN = Library of Congress Control Number

LCCN numbers are not required for you to publish your book; however, if you want your book available in libraries, you must apply for an LCCN number **BEFORE** you publish your book. CIP – Cataloging in Publication is only available for books that haven't been published. You can view a list of questions and answers regarding LCCN numbers at http://www.loc.gov/about/frequently-asked-questions/

1. ISBN = International Standard Book Number

This was easier to correct because of all the steps I took previously:

1. I changed <ol> at the beginning of each paragraph to <ol start="1"><li>, <ol start="2"><li>, <ol start="3"><li>, <ol start"=4"><li>, <ol start"=5"><li>, <ol start="6"><li>, <ol start= "7"><li>, <ol start="8"><li>, and <ol start= "9"><li>.

2. I removed </li> from the end of each line.

3. I removed <hr class="implicit-break" /> from the beginning of paragraphs 3 through 9.

4. I removed </p> from the end of paragraph 3 so paragraph 4 would align with the other paragraphs.

5. I removed <p class="first first-in-chapter first-full-width"> from in front of the 2nd paragraph under number 3 and replaced it with <ol> so it would align correctly, and then I added </ol> to the end of the paragraph. I repeated this for paragraphs 4, 5, 6, 7, 8, and 9.

6. I added <ol> before 6a and 6b, and then I added </ol> at the end of each of those so they'd both align correctly.

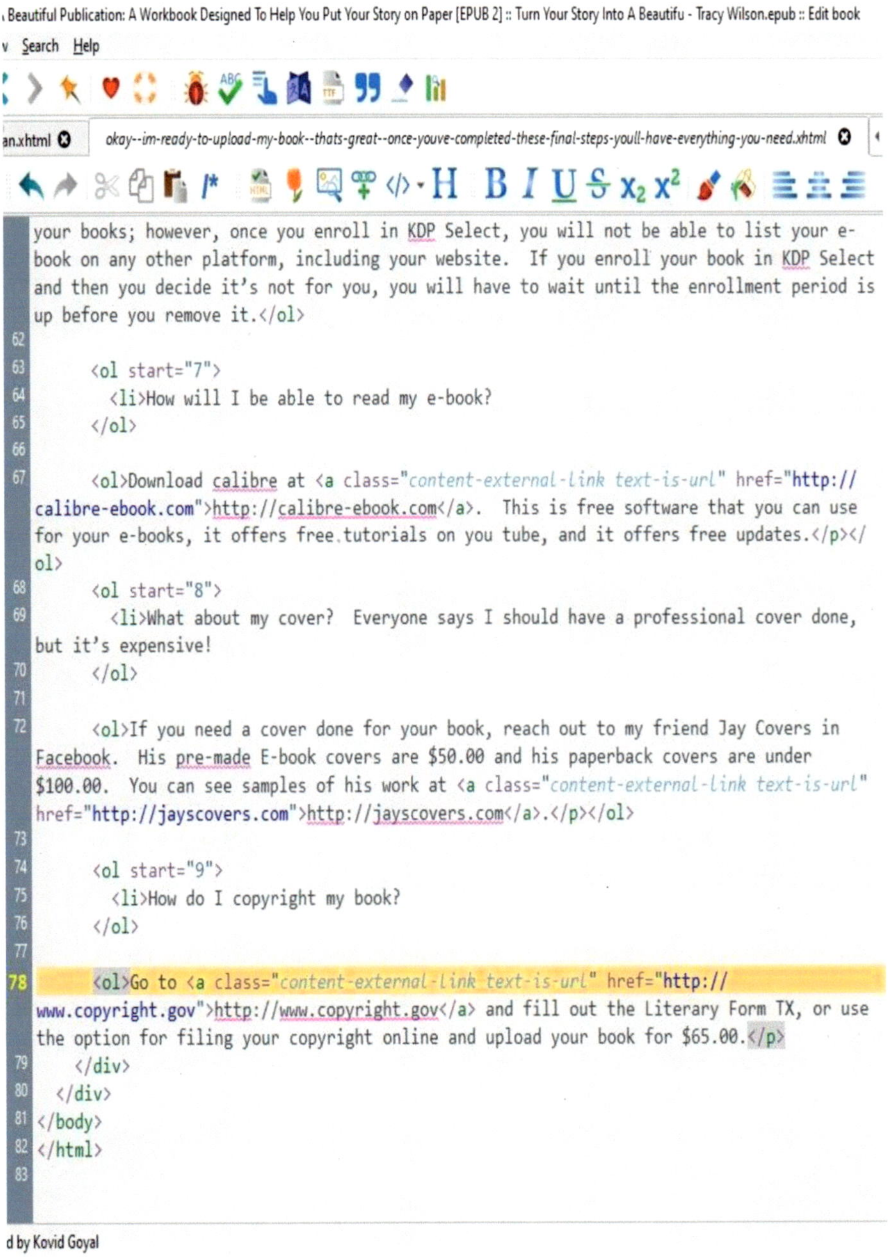


```
your books; however, once you enroll in KDP Select, you will not be able to list your e-book on any other platform, including your website.  If you enroll your book in KDP Select and then you decide it's not for you, you will have to wait until the enrollment period is up before you remove it.</ol>

      <ol start="7">
        <li>How will I be able to read my e-book?
      </ol>

      <ol>Download calibre at <a class="content-external-link text-is-url" href="http://calibre-ebook.com">http://calibre-ebook.com</a>.  This is free software that you can use for your e-books, it offers free tutorials on you tube, and it offers free updates.</p></ol>
      <ol start="8">
        <li>What about my cover?  Everyone says I should have a professional cover done, but it's expensive!
      </ol>

      <ol>If you need a cover done for your book, reach out to my friend Jay Covers in Facebook.  His pre-made E-book covers are $50.00 and his paperback covers are under $100.00.  You can see samples of his work at <a class="content-external-link text-is-url" href="http://jayscovers.com">http://jayscovers.com</a>.</p></ol>

      <ol start="9">
        <li>How do I copyright my book?
      </ol>

      <ol>Go to <a class="content-external-link text-is-url" href="http://www.copyright.gov">http://www.copyright.gov</a> and fill out the Literary Form TX, or use the option for filing your copyright online and upload your book for $65.00.</p>
    </div>
  </div>
</body>
</html>
```

File preview

"OKAY – I'M READY TO UPLOAD MY BOOK!" THAT'S GREAT! ONCE YOU'VE COMPLETED THESE FINAL STEPS, YOU'LL HAVE EVERYTHING YOU NEED!

1. Create a 2nd email account to use for your books. Don't use the same email account you use for social media or shopping on Amazon. You need to keep a separate account for your books.

2. Go to http://kdp.amazon.com and create an account with your second email. Follow the steps to fill in your tax information.

3. Copyright Page – this is an absolute must! If you don't know how to write a copyright page, google it to get a template or look at the copyright page in the front of this book. If your book is fiction, you

Search in preview

LATIN SMALL LETTER L : Line: 78 : 9

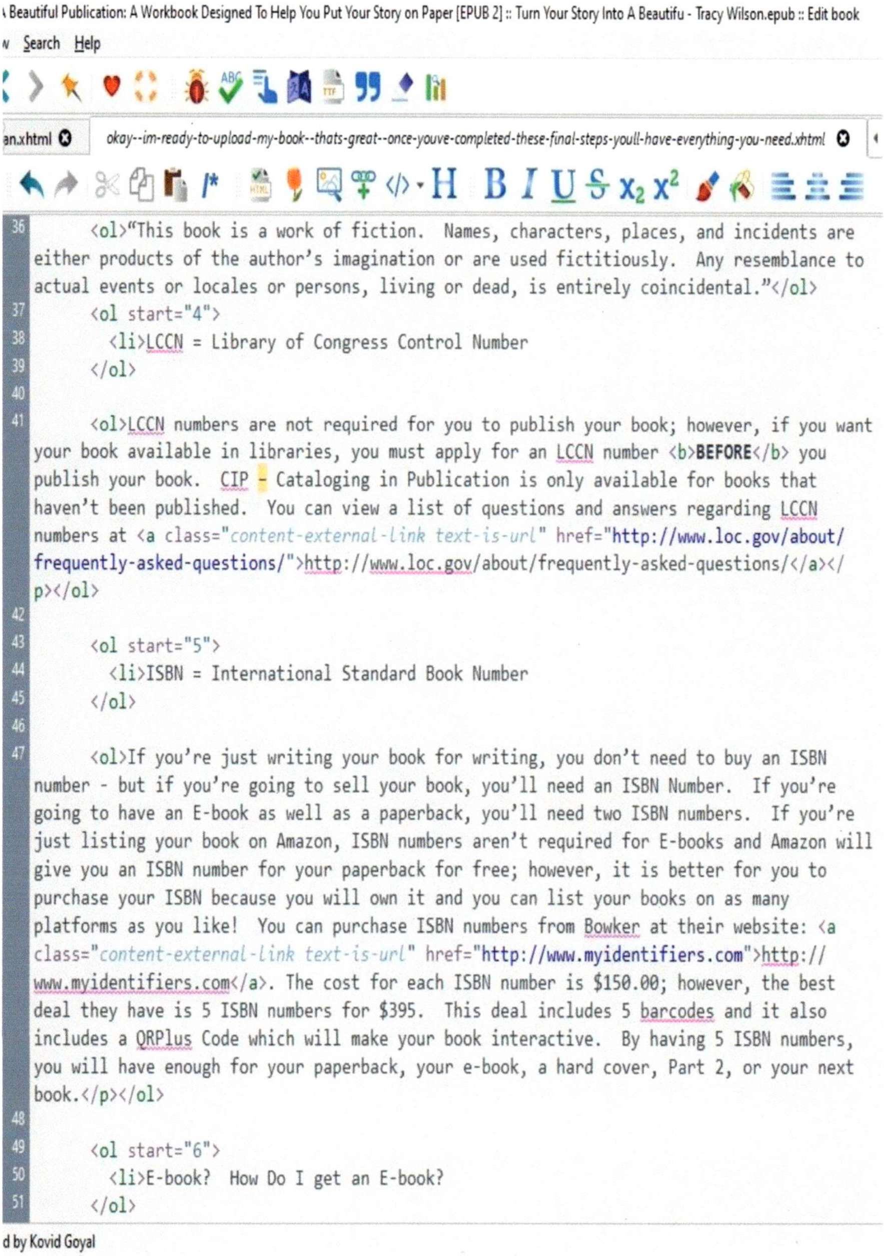


```
      <ol>"This book is a work of fiction.  Names, characters, places, and incidents are either products of the author's imagination or are used fictitiously.  Any resemblance to actual events or locales or persons, living or dead, is entirely coincidental."</ol>
      <ol start="4">
        <li>LCCN = Library of Congress Control Number
      </ol>

      <ol>LCCN numbers are not required for you to publish your book; however, if you want your book available in libraries, you must apply for an LCCN number <b>BEFORE</b> you publish your book.  CIP - Cataloging in Publication is only available for books that haven't been published.  You can view a list of questions and answers regarding LCCN numbers at <a class="content-external-link text-is-url" href="http://www.loc.gov/about/frequently-asked-questions/">http://www.loc.gov/about/frequently-asked-questions/</a></p></ol>

      <ol start="5">
        <li>ISBN = International Standard Book Number
      </ol>

      <ol>If you're just writing your book for writing, you don't need to buy an ISBN number - but if you're going to sell your book, you'll need an ISBN Number.  If you're going to have an E-book as well as a paperback, you'll need two ISBN numbers.  If you're just listing your book on Amazon, ISBN numbers aren't required for E-books and Amazon will give you an ISBN number for your paperback for free; however, it is better for you to purchase your ISBN because you will own it and you can list your books on as many platforms as you like!  You can purchase ISBN numbers from Bowker at their website: <a class="content-external-link text-is-url" href="http://www.myidentifiers.com">http://www.myidentifiers.com</a>. The cost for each ISBN number is $150.00; however, the best deal they have is 5 ISBN numbers for $395.  This deal includes 5 barcodes and it also includes a QRPlus Code which will make your book interactive.  By having 5 ISBN numbers, you will have enough for your paperback, your e-book, a hard cover, Part 2, or your next book.</p></ol>

      <ol start="6">
        <li>E-book?  How Do I get an E-book?
      </ol>
```

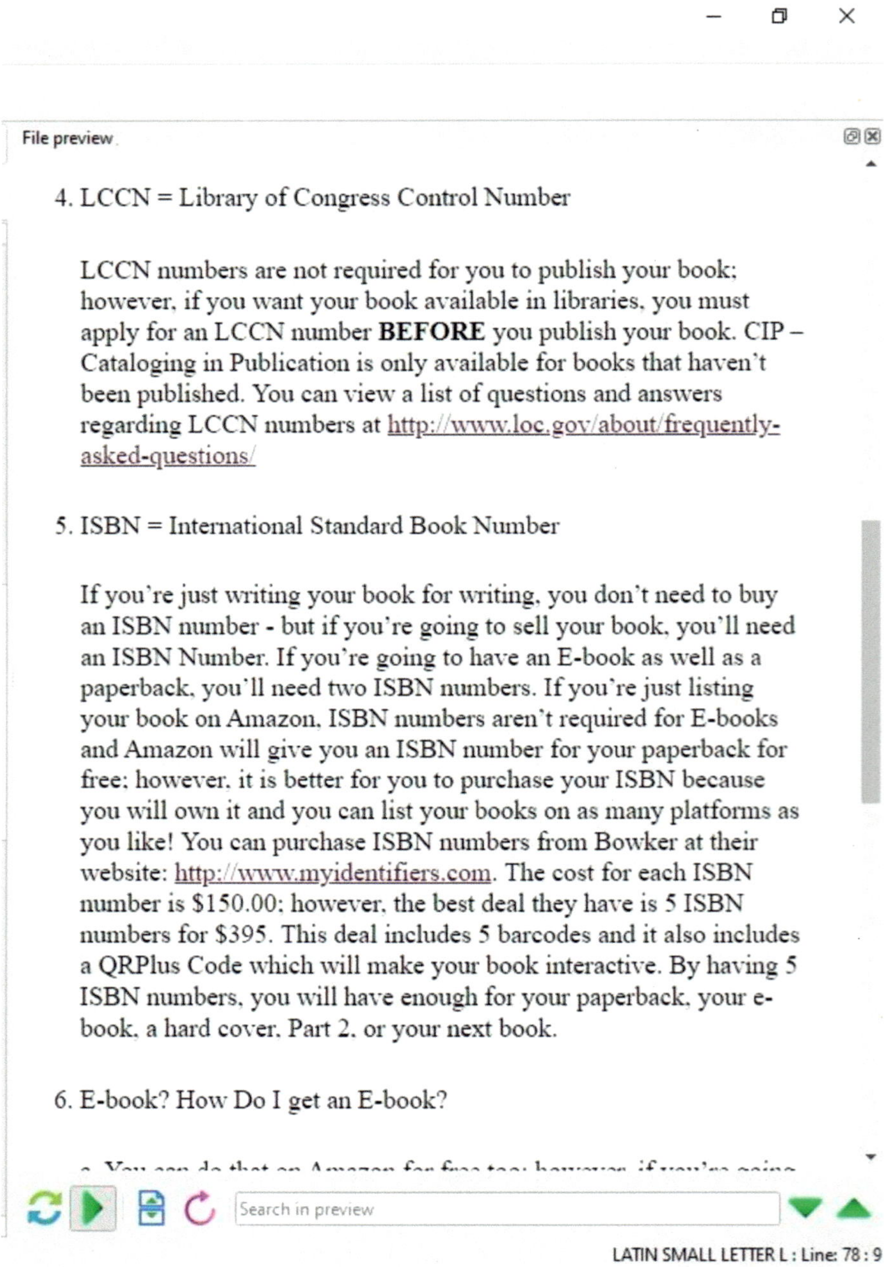

4. LCCN = Library of Congress Control Number

LCCN numbers are not required for you to publish your book; however, if you want your book available in libraries, you must apply for an LCCN number **BEFORE** you publish your book. CIP – Cataloging in Publication is only available for books that haven't been published. You can view a list of questions and answers regarding LCCN numbers at http://www.loc.gov/about/frequently-asked-questions/

5. ISBN = International Standard Book Number

If you're just writing your book for writing, you don't need to buy an ISBN number - but if you're going to sell your book, you'll need an ISBN Number. If you're going to have an E-book as well as a paperback, you'll need two ISBN numbers. If you're just listing your book on Amazon, ISBN numbers aren't required for E-books and Amazon will give you an ISBN number for your paperback for free; however, it is better for you to purchase your ISBN because you will own it and you can list your books on as many platforms as you like! You can purchase ISBN numbers from Bowker at their website: http://www.myidentifiers.com. The cost for each ISBN number is $150.00; however, the best deal they have is 5 ISBN numbers for $395. This deal includes 5 barcodes and it also includes a QRPlus Code which will make your book interactive. By having 5 ISBN numbers, you will have enough for your paperback, your e-book, a hard cover, Part 2, or your next book.

6. E-book? How Do I get an E-book?

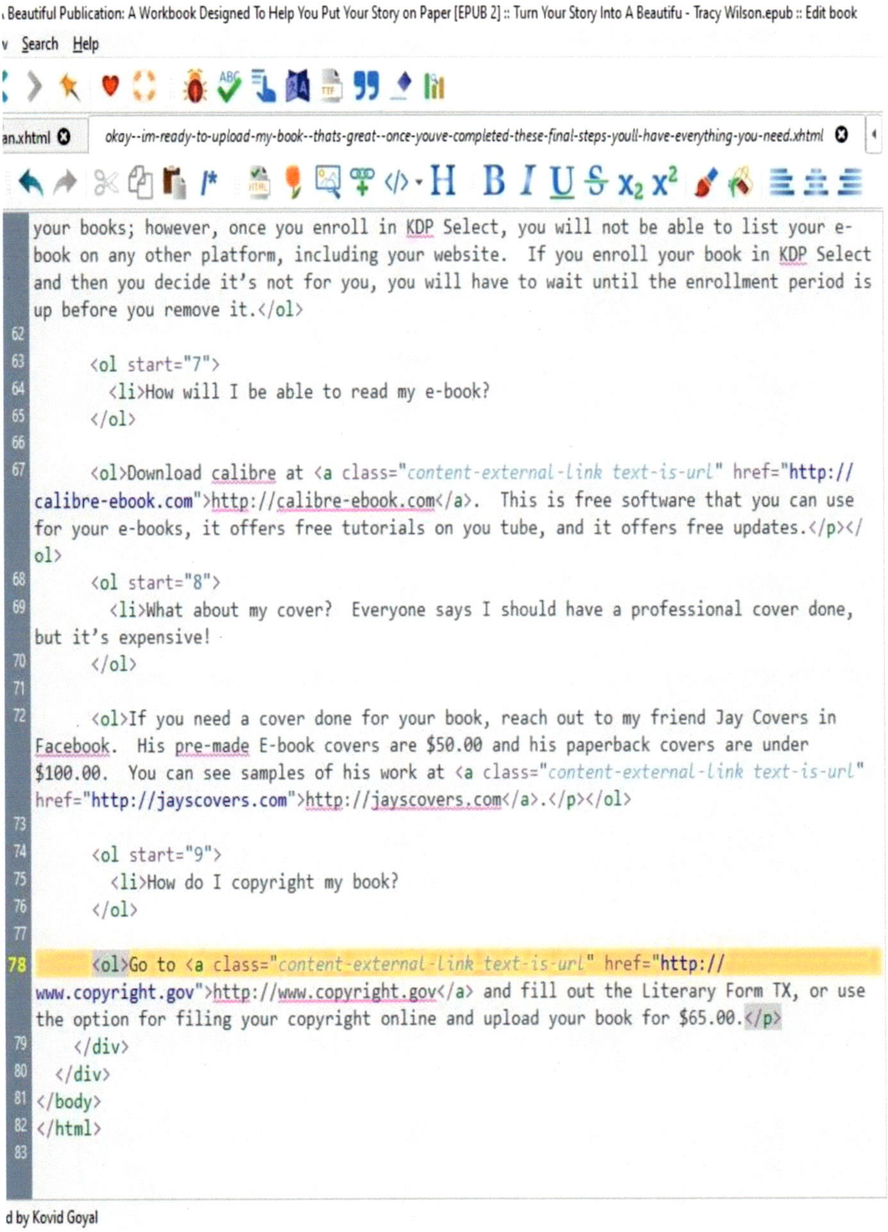


```
your books; however, once you enroll in KDP Select, you will not be able to list your e-book on any other platform, including your website.  If you enroll your book in KDP Select and then you decide it's not for you, you will have to wait until the enrollment period is up before you remove it.</ol>

      <ol start="7">
        <li>How will I be able to read my e-book?
      </ol>

      <ol>Download calibre at <a class="content-external-link text-is-url" href="http://calibre-ebook.com">http://calibre-ebook.com</a>.  This is free software that you can use for your e-books, it offers free tutorials on you tube, and it offers free updates.</p></ol>
      <ol start="8">
        <li>What about my cover?  Everyone says I should have a professional cover done, but it's expensive!
      </ol>

      <ol>If you need a cover done for your book, reach out to my friend Jay Covers in Facebook.  His pre-made E-book covers are $50.00 and his paperback covers are under $100.00.  You can see samples of his work at <a class="content-external-link text-is-url" href="http://jayscovers.com">http://jayscovers.com</a>.</p></ol>

      <ol start="9">
        <li>How do I copyright my book?
      </ol>

      <ol>Go to <a class="content-external-link text-is-url" href="http://www.copyright.gov">http://www.copyright.gov</a> and fill out the Literary Form TX, or use the option for filing your copyright online and upload your book for $65.00.</p>
    </div>
  </div>
</body>
</html>
```

File preview

b. KDP Select

This is a program that allows readers that have Kindle Unlimited to read your books without purchasing them. This gives you an opportunity to earn higher royalties on your books; however, once you enroll in KDP Select, you will not be able to list your e-book on any other platform, including your website. If you enroll your book in KDP Select and then you decide it's not for you, you will have to wait until the enrollment period is up before you remove it.

7. How will I be able to read my e-book?

Download calibre at http://calibre-ebook.com. This is free software that you can use for your e-books, it offers free tutorials on you tube, and it offers free updates.

8. What about my cover? Everyone says I should have a professional cover done, but it's expensive!

If you need a cover done for your book, reach out to my friend Jay Covers in Facebook. His pre-made E-book covers are $50.00 and his paperback covers are under $100.00. You can see samples of his work at http://jayscovers.com.

9. How do I copyright my book?

Go to http://www.copyright.gov and fill out the Literary Form TX, or use the option for filing your copyright online and upload your book for $65.00.

Search in preview

LATIN SMALL LETTER L : Line: 78 : 9

When I got to ‘I Want To Print My Book In Color’ I saw the following:

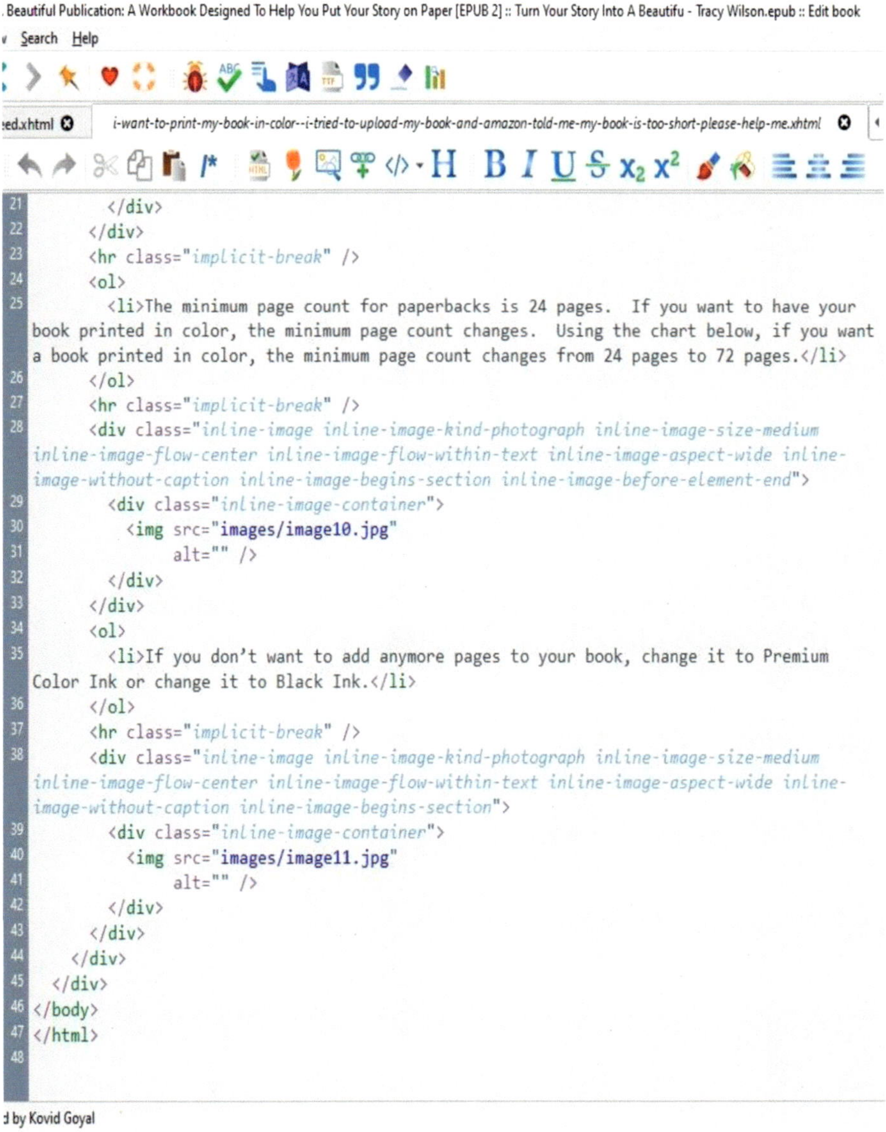


```
        </div>
      </div>
      <hr class="implicit-break" />
      <ol>
        <li>The minimum page count for paperbacks is 24 pages.  If you want to have your book printed in color, the minimum page count changes.  Using the chart below, if you want a book printed in color, the minimum page count changes from 24 pages to 72 pages.</li>
      </ol>
      <hr class="implicit-break" />
      <div class="inline-image inline-image-kind-photograph inline-image-size-medium inline-image-flow-center inline-image-flow-within-text inline-image-aspect-wide inline-image-without-caption inline-image-begins-section inline-image-before-element-end">
        <div class="inline-image-container">
          <img src="images/image10.jpg"
               alt="" />
        </div>
      </div>
      <ol>
        <li>If you don’t want to add anymore pages to your book, change it to Premium Color Ink or change it to Black Ink.</li>
      </ol>
      <hr class="implicit-break" />
      <div class="inline-image inline-image-kind-photograph inline-image-size-medium inline-image-flow-center inline-image-flow-within-text inline-image-aspect-wide inline-image-without-caption inline-image-begins-section">
        <div class="inline-image-container">
          <img src="images/image11.jpg"
               alt="" />
        </div>
      </div>
    </div>
  </div>
</body>
</html>
```

File preview

1. The minimum page count for paperbacks is 24 pages. If you want to have your book printed in color, the minimum page count changes. Using the chart below, if you want a book printed in color, the minimum page count changes from 24 pages to 72 pages.

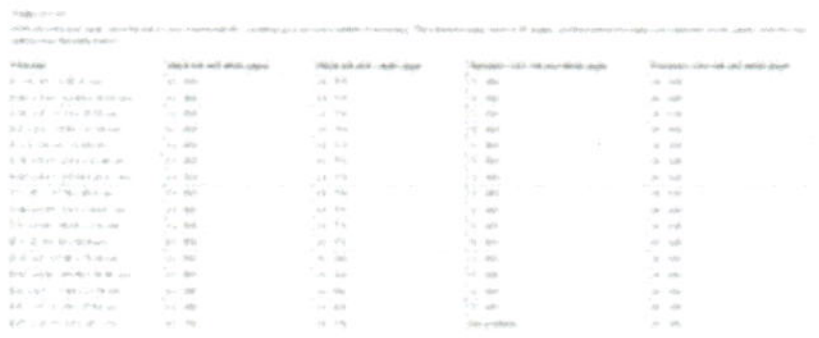

1. If you don't want to add anymore pages to your book, change it to Premium Color Ink or change it to Black Ink.

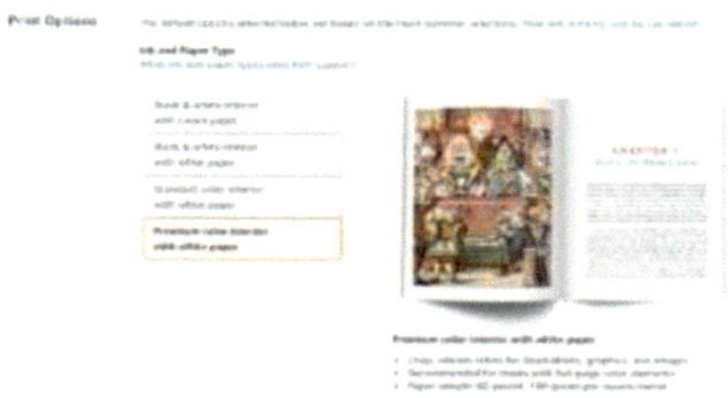

Search in preview

Line: 1 : 0

I changed <ol> to <ol start="1">, <ol start="2">.

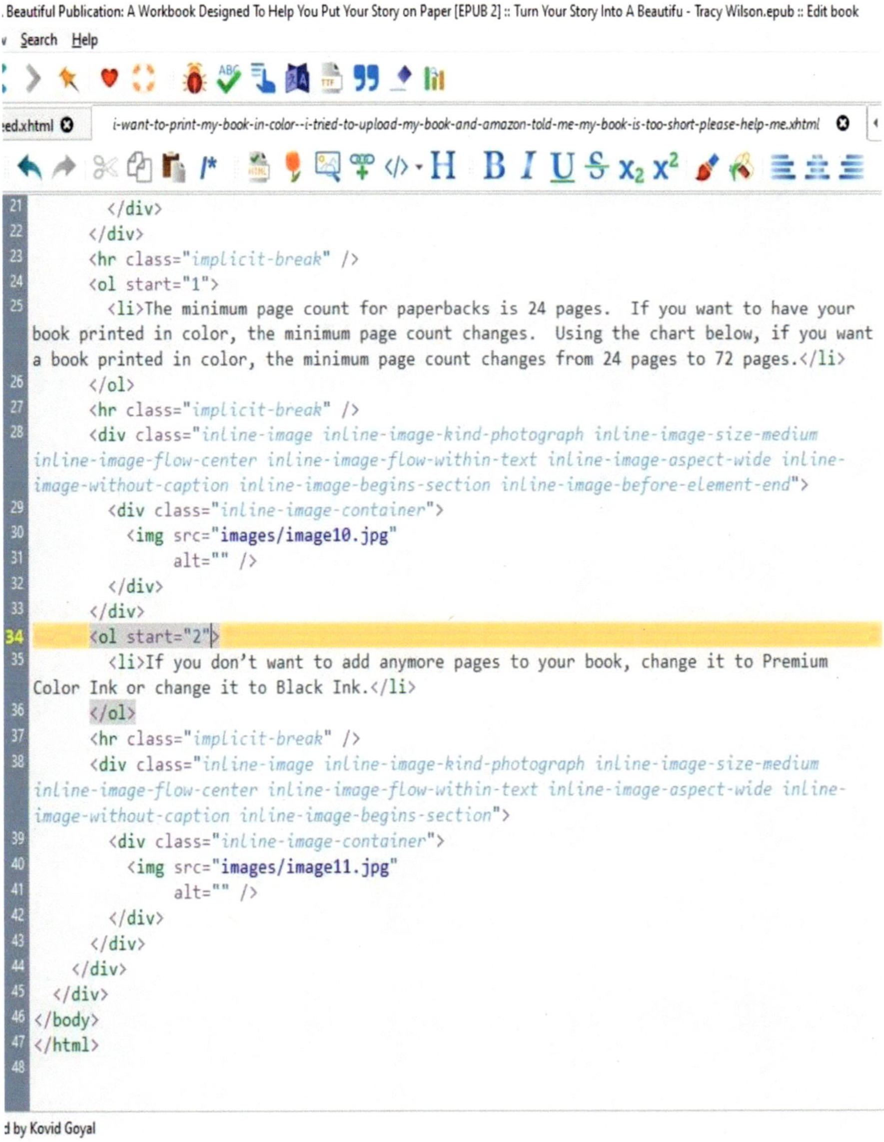

File preview

1. The minimum page count for paperbacks is 24 pages. If you want to have your book printed in color, the minimum page count changes. Using the chart below, if you want a book printed in color, the minimum page count changes from 24 pages to 72 pages.

2. If you don't want to add anymore pages to your book, change it to Premium Color Ink or change it to Black Ink.

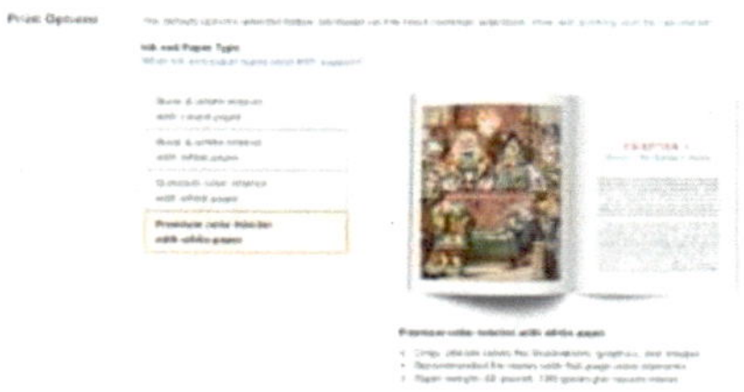

Search in preview

QUOTATION MARK : Line: 34 : 19

When I got to 'My Friends & Family Want Printed Copies' I saw the following:

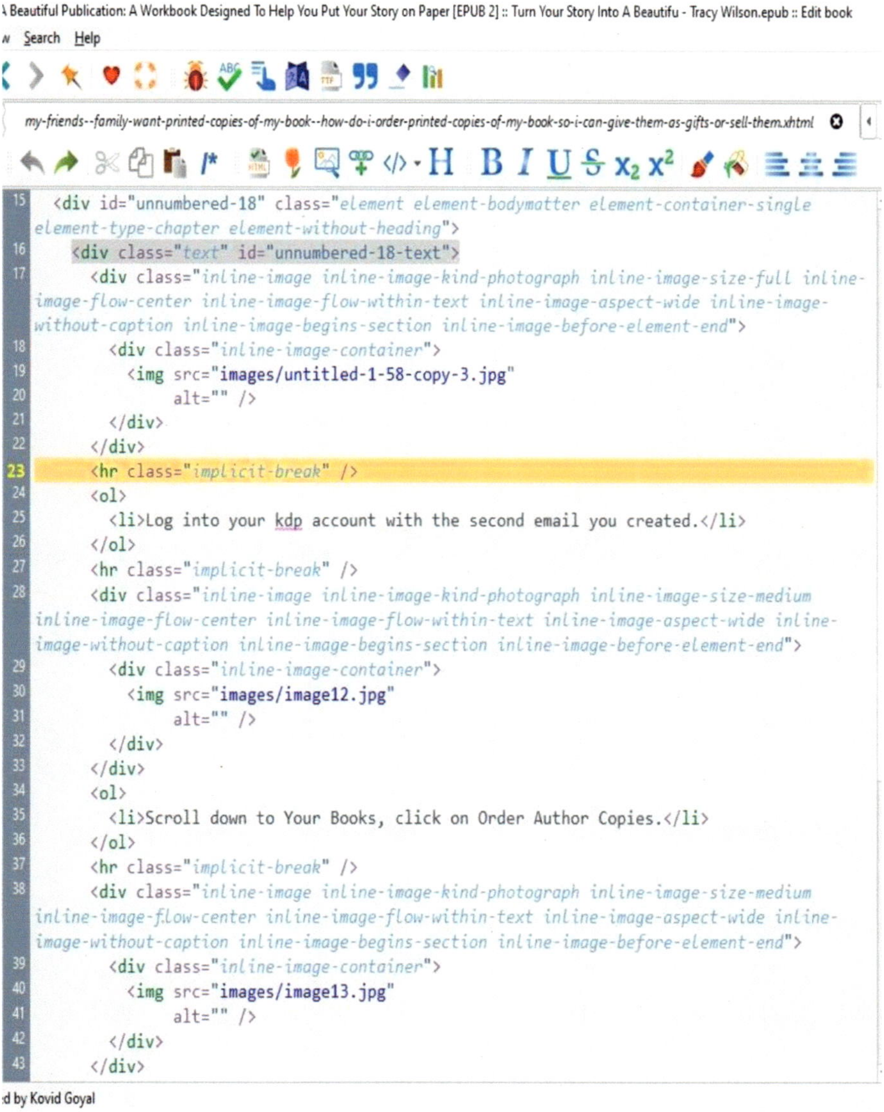


```
  <div id="unnumbered-18" class="element element-bodymatter element-container-single element-type-chapter element-without-heading">
    <div class="text" id="unnumbered-18-text">
      <div class="inline-image inline-image-kind-photograph inline-image-size-full inline-image-flow-center inline-image-flow-within-text inline-image-aspect-wide inline-image-without-caption inline-image-begins-section inline-image-before-element-end">
        <div class="inline-image-container">
          <img src="images/untitled-1-58-copy-3.jpg"
              alt="" />
        </div>
      </div>
      <hr class="implicit-break" />
      <ol>
        <li>Log into your kdp account with the second email you created.</li>
      </ol>
      <hr class="implicit-break" />
      <div class="inline-image inline-image-kind-photograph inline-image-size-medium inline-image-flow-center inline-image-flow-within-text inline-image-aspect-wide inline-image-without-caption inline-image-begins-section inline-image-before-element-end">
        <div class="inline-image-container">
          <img src="images/image12.jpg"
              alt="" />
        </div>
      </div>
      <ol>
        <li>Scroll down to Your Books, click on Order Author Copies.</li>
      </ol>
      <hr class="implicit-break" />
      <div class="inline-image inline-image-kind-photograph inline-image-size-medium inline-image-flow-center inline-image-flow-within-text inline-image-aspect-wide inline-image-without-caption inline-image-begins-section inline-image-before-element-end">
        <div class="inline-image-container">
          <img src="images/image13.jpg"
              alt="" />
        </div>
      </div>
```

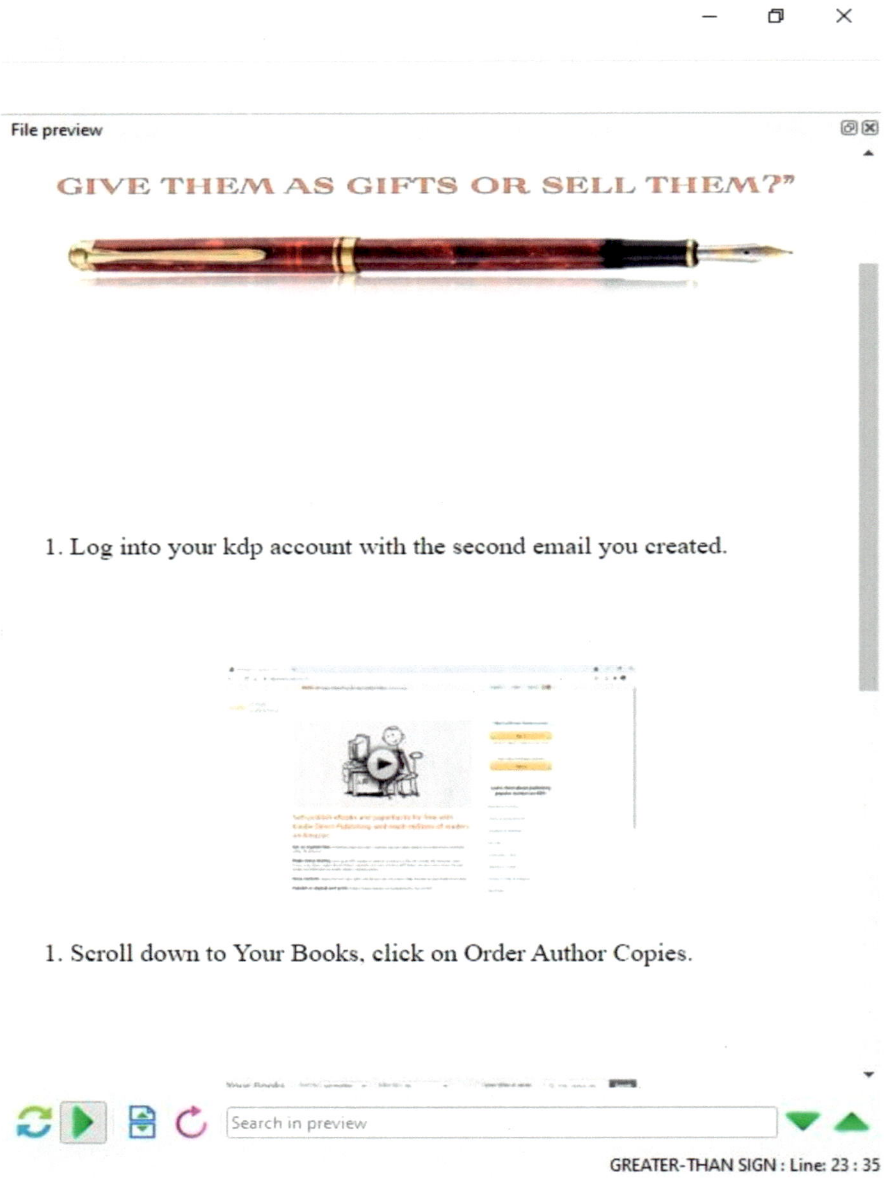
File preview
GIVE THEM AS GIFTS OR SELL THEM?"
1. Log into your kdp account with the second email you created.
1. Scroll down to Your Books, click on Order Author Copies.
Search in preview
GREATER-THAN SIGN : Line: 23 : 35

Beautiful Publication: A Workbook Designed To Help You Put Your Story on Paper [EPUB 2] :: Turn Your Story Into A Beautifu - Tracy Wilson.epub :: Edit book

Search Help

my-friends--family-want-printed-copies-of-my-book--how-do-i-order-printed-copies-of-my-book-so-i-can-give-them-as-gifts-or-sell-them.xhtml

```
        <li>Scroll down to Your Books, click on Order Author Copies.</li>
      </ol>
      <hr class="implicit-break" />
      <div class="inline-image inline-image-kind-photograph inline-image-size-medium inline-image-flow-center inline-image-flow-within-text inline-image-aspect-wide inline-image-without-caption inline-image-begins-section inline-image-before-element-end">
        <div class="inline-image-container">
          <img src="images/image13.jpg"
               alt="" />
        </div>
      </div>
      <hr class="implicit-break" />
      <ol>
        <li>Fill in the number of author copies you want, change the market place to amazon.com, and click submit.</li>
      </ol>
      <hr class="implicit-break" />
      <div class="inline-image inline-image-kind-photograph inline-image-size-medium inline-image-flow-center inline-image-flow-within-text inline-image-aspect-wide inline-image-without-caption inline-image-begins-section inline-image-before-element-end">
        <div class="inline-image-container">
          <img src="images/image14.jpg"
               alt="" />
        </div>
      </div>
      <hr class="implicit-break" />
      <ol>
        <li>You will receive an email in your second email account letting you know when your copies are in your shopping cart.</li>
      </ol>
    </div>
  </div>
</body>
</html>
```

l by Kovid Goyal

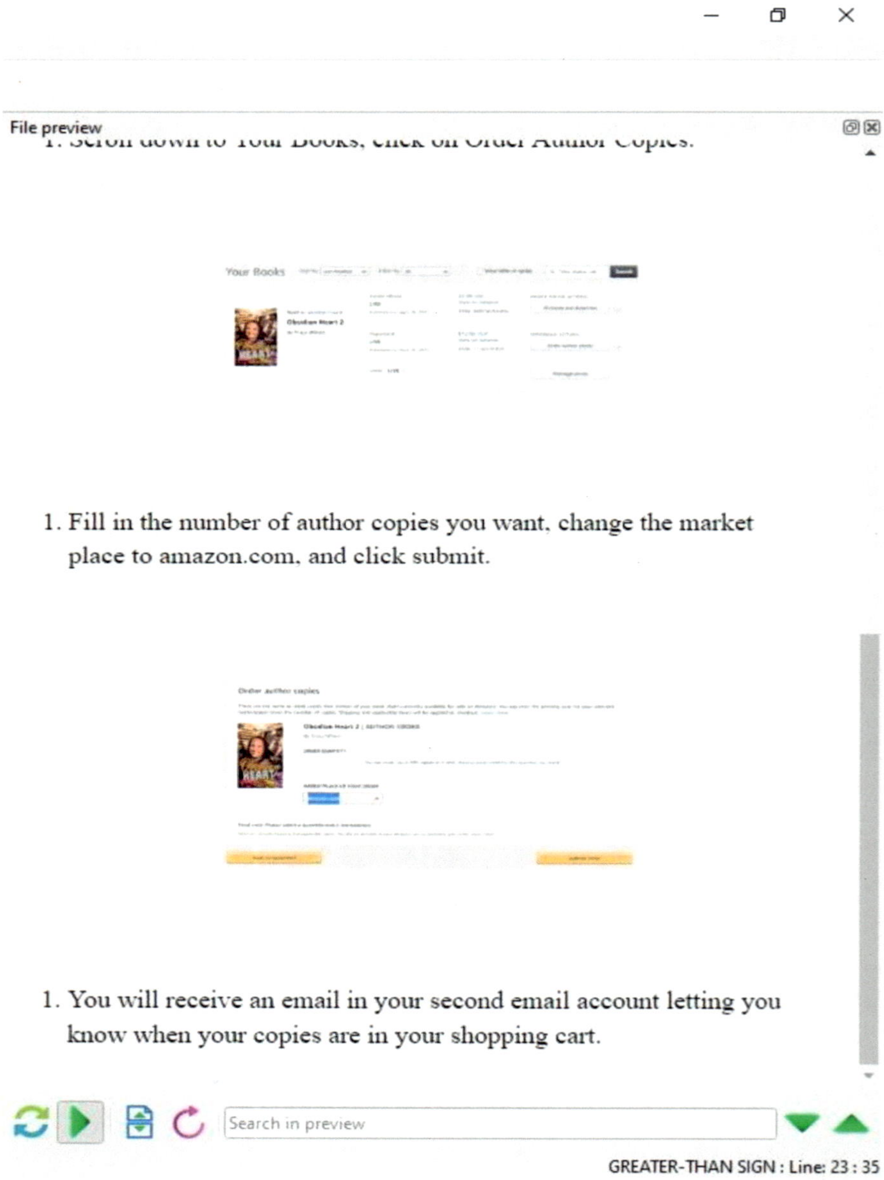
File preview
Your Books
Obsidian Heart 2
Order author copies
1. Fill in the number of author copies you want, change the market place to amazon.com, and click submit.
1. You will receive an email in your second email account letting you know when your copies are in your shopping cart.
Search in preview
GREATER-THAN SIGN : Line: 23 : 35

I changed <ol> to <ol start="1">, <ol start="2">, <ol> to <ol start="3">, <ol start="4">.

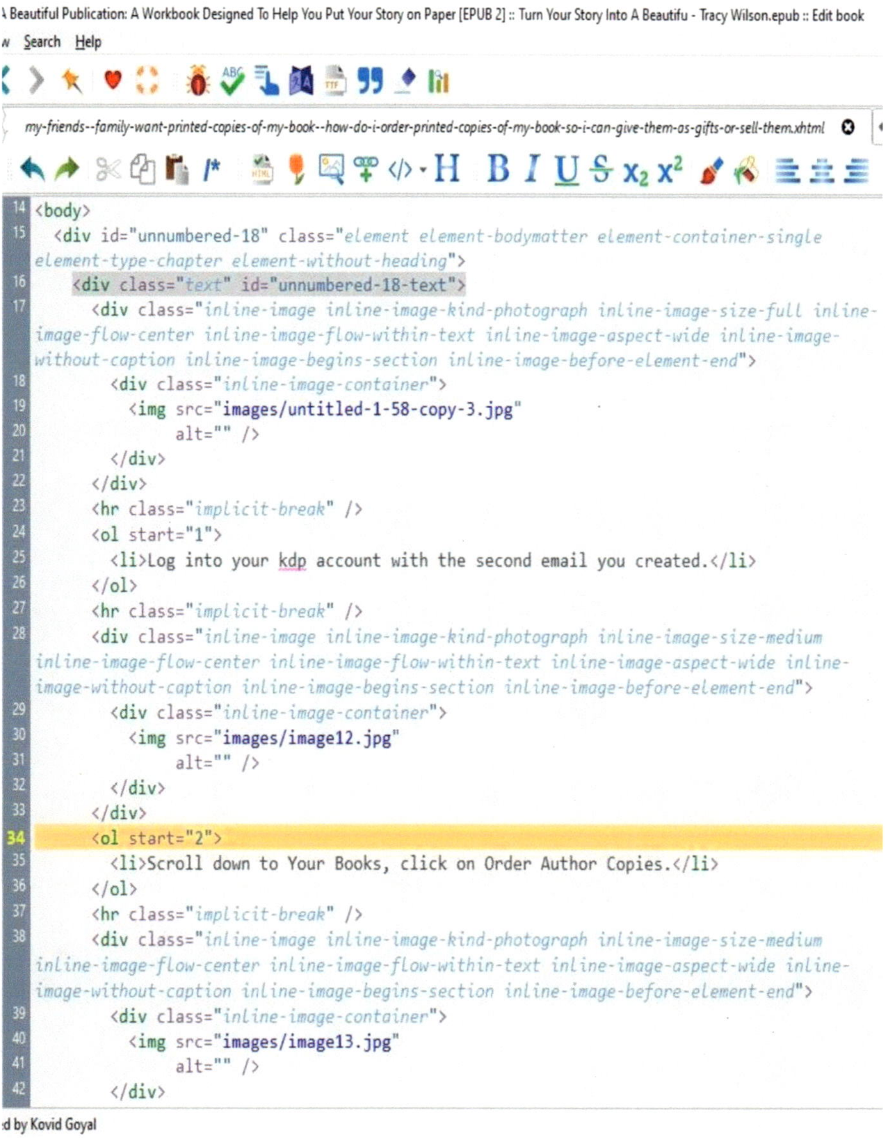


```
<body>
  <div id="unnumbered-18" class="element element-bodymatter element-container-single
element-type-chapter element-without-heading">
    <div class="text" id="unnumbered-18-text">
      <div class="inline-image inline-image-kind-photograph inline-image-size-full inline-
image-flow-center inline-image-flow-within-text inline-image-aspect-wide inline-image-
without-caption inline-image-begins-section inline-image-before-element-end">
        <div class="inline-image-container">
          <img src="images/untitled-1-58-copy-3.jpg"
               alt="" />
        </div>
      </div>
      <hr class="implicit-break" />
      <ol start="1">
        <li>Log into your kdp account with the second email you created.</li>
      </ol>
      <hr class="implicit-break" />
      <div class="inline-image inline-image-kind-photograph inline-image-size-medium
inline-image-flow-center inline-image-flow-within-text inline-image-aspect-wide inline-
image-without-caption inline-image-begins-section inline-image-before-element-end">
        <div class="inline-image-container">
          <img src="images/image12.jpg"
               alt="" />
        </div>
      </div>
      <ol start="2">
        <li>Scroll down to Your Books, click on Order Author Copies.</li>
      </ol>
      <hr class="implicit-break" />
      <div class="inline-image inline-image-kind-photograph inline-image-size-medium
inline-image-flow-center inline-image-flow-within-text inline-image-aspect-wide inline-
image-without-caption inline-image-begins-section inline-image-before-element-end">
        <div class="inline-image-container">
          <img src="images/image13.jpg"
               alt="" />
        </div>
```

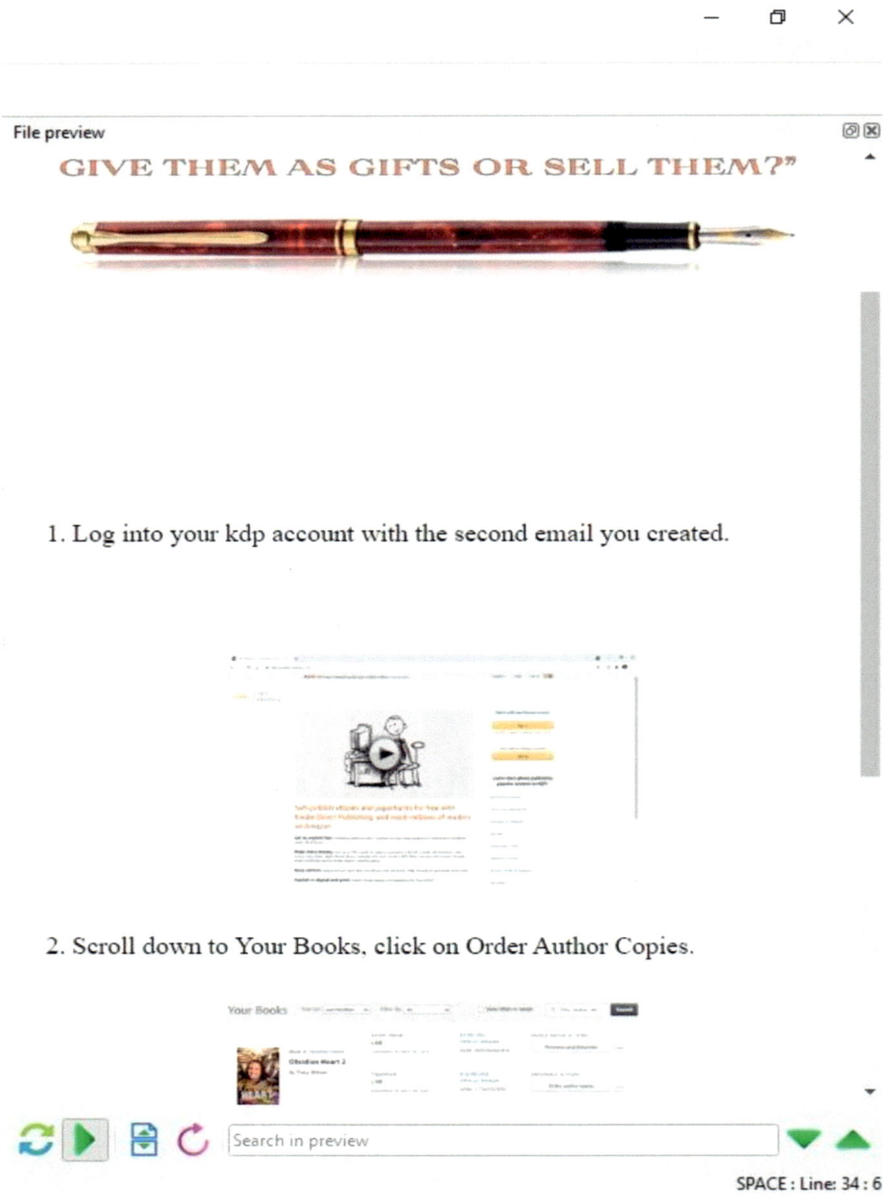
File preview
GIVE THEM AS GIFTS OR SELL THEM?"
1. Log into your kdp account with the second email you created.
2. Scroll down to Your Books, click on Order Author Copies.
Your Books
Search in preview
SPACE : Line: 34 : 6

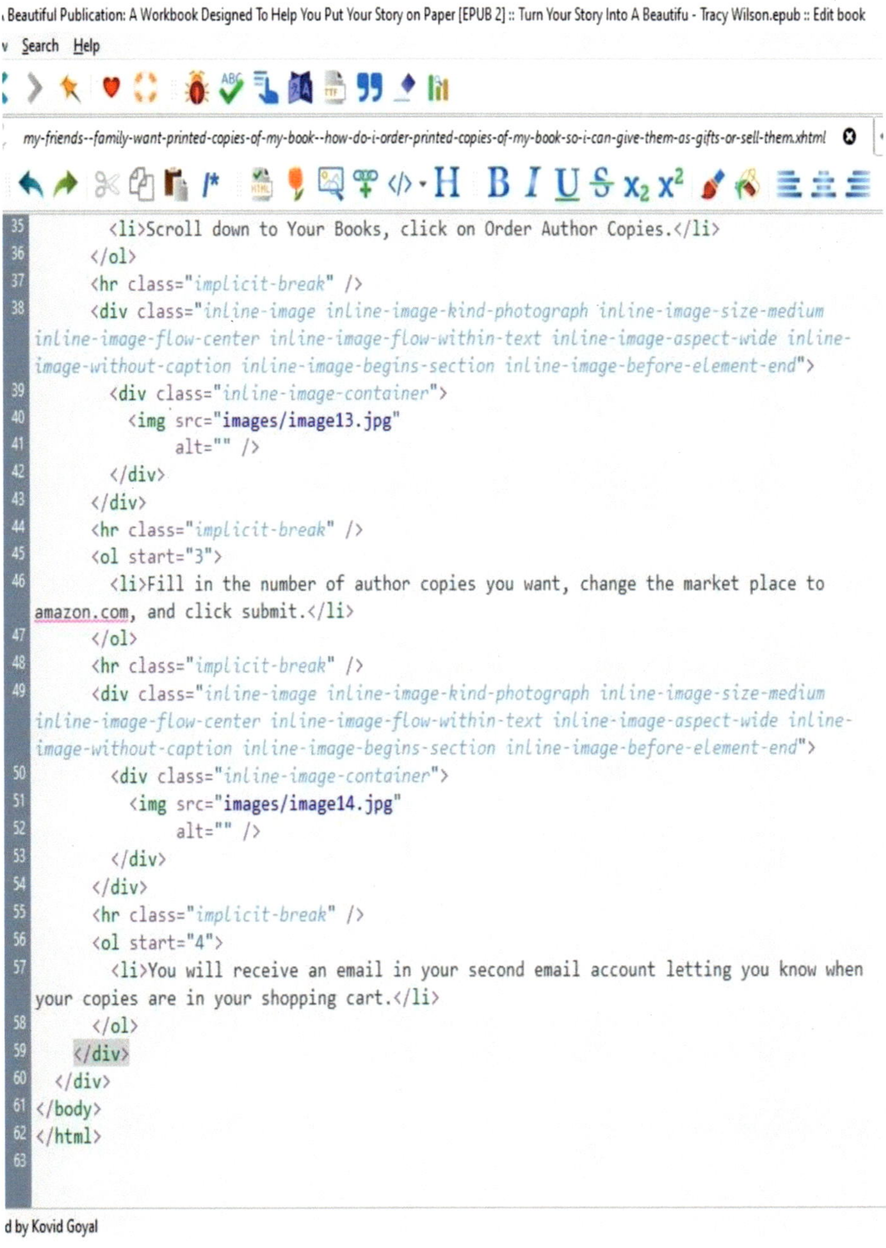


```
        <li>Scroll down to Your Books, click on Order Author Copies.</li>
      </ol>
      <hr class="implicit-break" />
      <div class="inline-image inline-image-kind-photograph inline-image-size-medium inline-image-flow-center inline-image-flow-within-text inline-image-aspect-wide inline-image-without-caption inline-image-begins-section inline-image-before-element-end">
        <div class="inline-image-container">
          <img src="images/image13.jpg"
               alt="" />
        </div>
      </div>
      <hr class="implicit-break" />
      <ol start="3">
        <li>Fill in the number of author copies you want, change the market place to amazon.com, and click submit.</li>
      </ol>
      <hr class="implicit-break" />
      <div class="inline-image inline-image-kind-photograph inline-image-size-medium inline-image-flow-center inline-image-flow-within-text inline-image-aspect-wide inline-image-without-caption inline-image-begins-section inline-image-before-element-end">
        <div class="inline-image-container">
          <img src="images/image14.jpg"
               alt="" />
        </div>
      </div>
      <hr class="implicit-break" />
      <ol start="4">
        <li>You will receive an email in your second email account letting you know when your copies are in your shopping cart.</li>
      </ol>
    </div>
  </div>
</body>
</html>
```

File preview

2. Scroll down to Your Books, click on Order Author Copies.

3. Fill in the number of author copies you want, change the market place to amazon.com, and click submit.

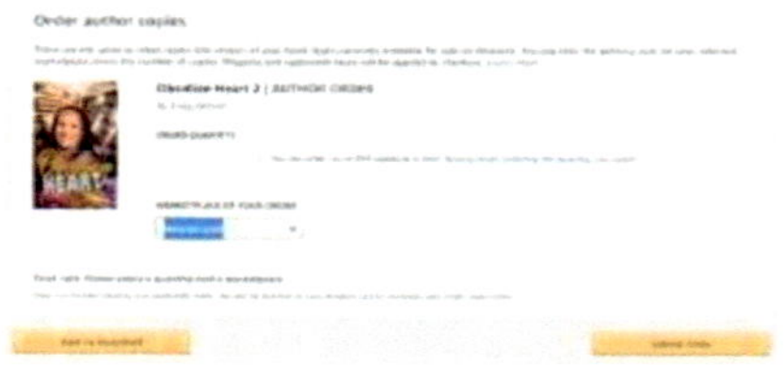

4. You will receive an email in your second email account letting you know when your copies are in your shopping cart.

Search in preview

SPACE : Line: 34 : 6

When I got to 'How Do I Let Everyone Know My Book Is Available' I saw the following:

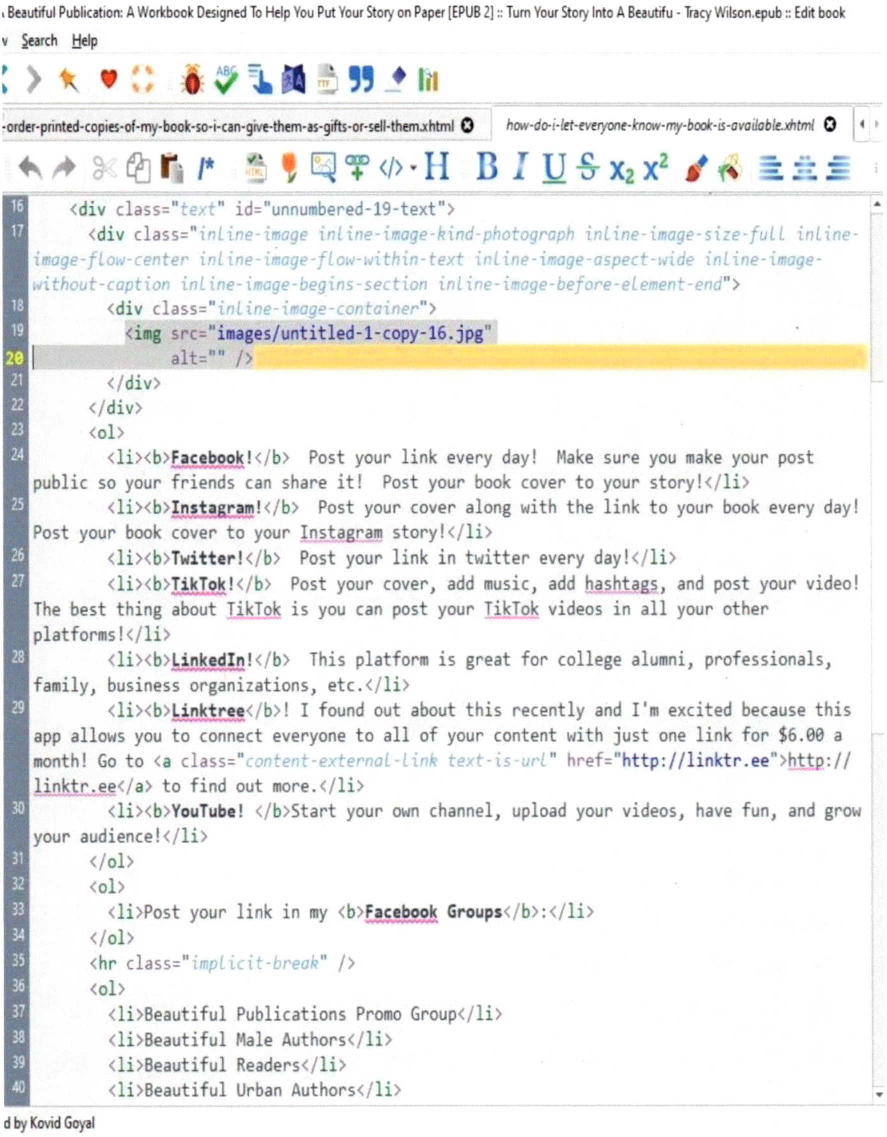


```
<div class="text" id="unnumbered-19-text">
  <div class="inline-image inline-image-kind-photograph inline-image-size-full inline-image-flow-center inline-image-flow-within-text inline-image-aspect-wide inline-image-without-caption inline-image-begins-section inline-image-before-element-end">
    <div class="inline-image-container">
      <img src="images/untitled-1-copy-16.jpg"
         alt="" />
    </div>
  </div>
  <ol>
    <li><b>Facebook!</b>  Post your link every day!  Make sure you make your post public so your friends can share it!  Post your book cover to your story!</li>
    <li><b>Instagram!</b>  Post your cover along with the link to your book every day! Post your book cover to your Instagram story!</li>
    <li><b>Twitter!</b>  Post your link in twitter every day!</li>
    <li><b>TikTok!</b>  Post your cover, add music, add hashtags, and post your video! The best thing about TikTok is you can post your TikTok videos in all your other platforms!</li>
    <li><b>LinkedIn!</b>  This platform is great for college alumni, professionals, family, business organizations, etc.</li>
    <li><b>Linktree</b>! I found out about this recently and I'm excited because this app allows you to connect everyone to all of your content with just one link for $6.00 a month! Go to <a class="content-external-link text-is-url" href="http://linktr.ee">http://linktr.ee</a> to find out more.</li>
    <li><b>YouTube! </b>Start your own channel, upload your videos, have fun, and grow your audience!</li>
  </ol>
  <ol>
    <li>Post your link in my <b>Facebook Groups</b>:</li>
  </ol>
  <hr class="implicit-break" />
  <ol>
    <li>Beautiful Publications Promo Group</li>
    <li>Beautiful Male Authors</li>
    <li>Beautiful Readers</li>
    <li>Beautiful Urban Authors</li>
```

1. **Facebook!** Post your link every day! Make sure you make your post public so your friends can share it! Post your book cover to your story!
2. **Instagram!** Post your cover along with the link to your book every day! Post your book cover to your Instagram story!
3. **Twitter!** Post your link in twitter every day!
4. **TikTok!** Post your cover, add music, add hashtags, and post your video! The best thing about TikTok is you can post your TikTok videos in all your other platforms!
5. **LinkedIn!** This platform is great for college alumni, professionals, family, business organizations, etc.
6. **Linktree**! I found out about this recently and I'm excited because this app allows you to connect everyone to all of your content with just one link for $6.00 a month! Go to http://linktr.ee to find out more.
7. **YouTube!** Start your own channel, upload your videos, have fun, and grow your audience!

1. Post your link in my **Facebook Groups**:

1. Beautiful Publications Promo Group
2. Beautiful Male Authors
3. Beautiful Readers
4. Beautiful Urban Authors

Beautiful Publication: A Workbook Designed To Help You Put Your Story on Paper [EPUB 2] :: Turn Your Story Into A Beautifu - Tracy Wilson.epub :: Edit book

v Search Help

-order-printed-copies-of-my-book-so-i-can-give-them-as-gifts-or-sell-them.xhtml

how-do-i-let-everyone-know-my-book-is-available.xhtml

```
        <li>Beautiful Urban Authors</li>
        <li>Beautiful Urban Paperbacks</li>
        <li>Beautiful Urban Best Sellers</li>
        <li>Beautiful Urban Indies</li>
        <li>Beautiful Urban Kindles</li>
        <li>Beautiful Urban Standalones</li>
      </ol>
      <hr class="implicit-break" />
      <ol>
        <li>Get in <b>Clubhouse</b>!</li>
      </ol>
      <hr class="implicit-break" />
      <p class="first first-in-chapter first-full-width">Android users are allowed on the platform now and Clubhouse is lit!  There are clubs for you to do anything and everything from promoting your book, making friends, networking, getting your books in libraries, podcasting, following celebrities, etc.!  The best thing about clubhouse is once you create your profile all you need to do is the following:</p>
      <hr class="implicit-break" />
      <ol>
        <li>Make sure you use the cover of your book as your profile picture.</li>
        <li>Let everyone know where they can purchase your book.</li>
        <li>Link your Twitter and your Instagram to your clubhouse account.</li>
        <li>Join my clubhouse group, Beautiful Readers.  We meet on Saturdays at 6 p.m. EST.  Come into the room and talk about your book.</li>
      </ol>
      <p class="first first-in-section first-full-width">Each time you go into a room and you click on the little hand to ask a question, you get moved up into the top of the room. Once this happens, people will click on your profile and you'll get followers!  If you need an invite, post a status asking your friends if they have an invite or PM Beautiee Tracy Wilson to get one!</p>
    </div>
  </div>
</body>
</html>
```

d by Kovid Goyal

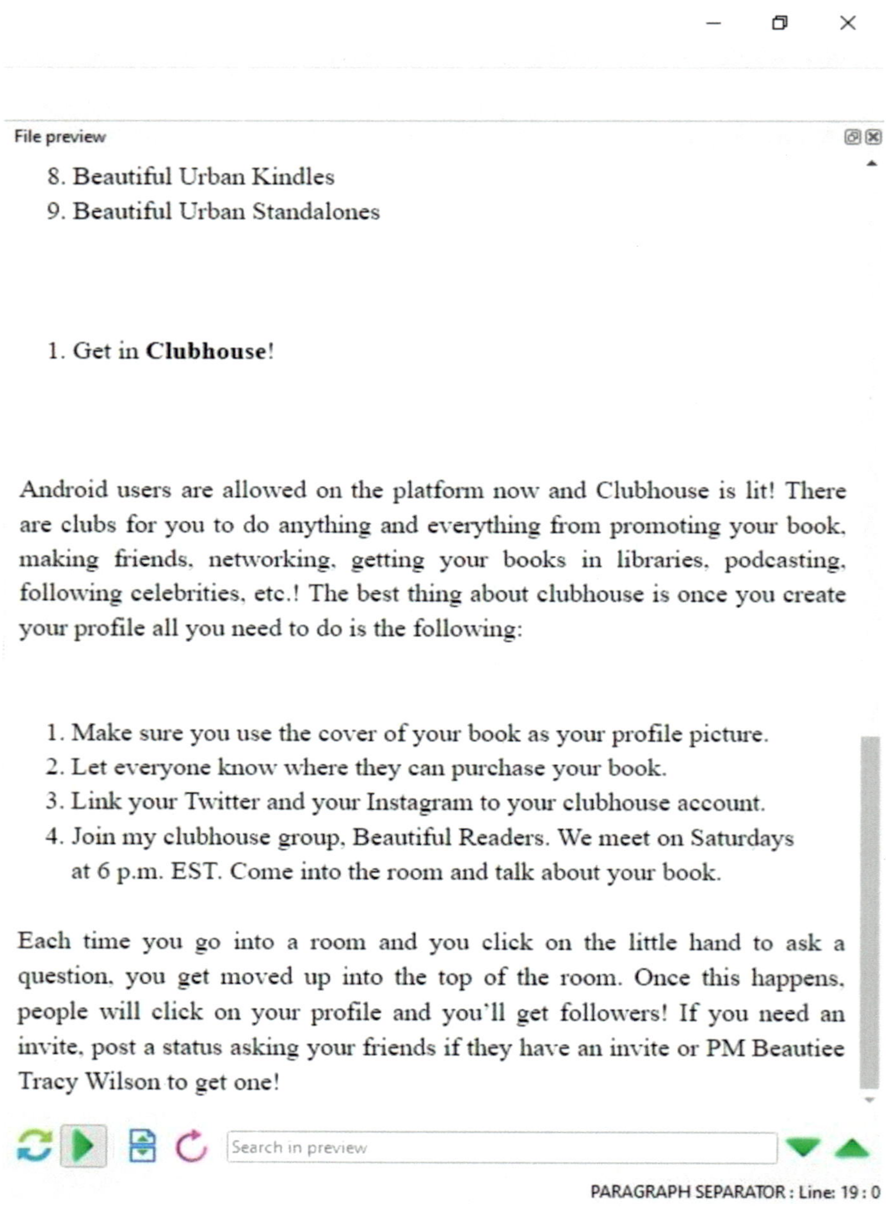

8. Beautiful Urban Kindles
9. Beautiful Urban Standalones

1. Get in **Clubhouse**!

Android users are allowed on the platform now and Clubhouse is lit! There are clubs for you to do anything and everything from promoting your book, making friends, networking, getting your books in libraries, podcasting, following celebrities, etc.! The best thing about clubhouse is once you create your profile all you need to do is the following:

1. Make sure you use the cover of your book as your profile picture.
2. Let everyone know where they can purchase your book.
3. Link your Twitter and your Instagram to your clubhouse account.
4. Join my clubhouse group, Beautiful Readers. We meet on Saturdays at 6 p.m. EST. Come into the room and talk about your book.

Each time you go into a room and you click on the little hand to ask a question, you get moved up into the top of the room. Once this happens, people will click on your profile and you'll get followers! If you need an invite, post a status asking your friends if they have an invite or PM Beautiee Tracy Wilson to get one!

1. I changed <ol> to <ol start="8">, starting with number 8.

2. I removed <li> before and </li> after all the groups, changed the listing to a, b, c, d, e, f, g, h, i, and I also added <p> at the end of each line to put them on a separate line and have them line up correctly.

3. I removed <hr class="implicit-break" /> from the top of the groups to move it up the page.

4. I removed <hr class="implicit-break" /> from the beginning and the end of the line, Clubhouse.

5. I removed <p class="first first-in-chapter first-full-width"> from the beginning of the first paragraph under clubhouse.

6. I removed <li> before and </li> after each line and changed the listing to a, b, c, d.

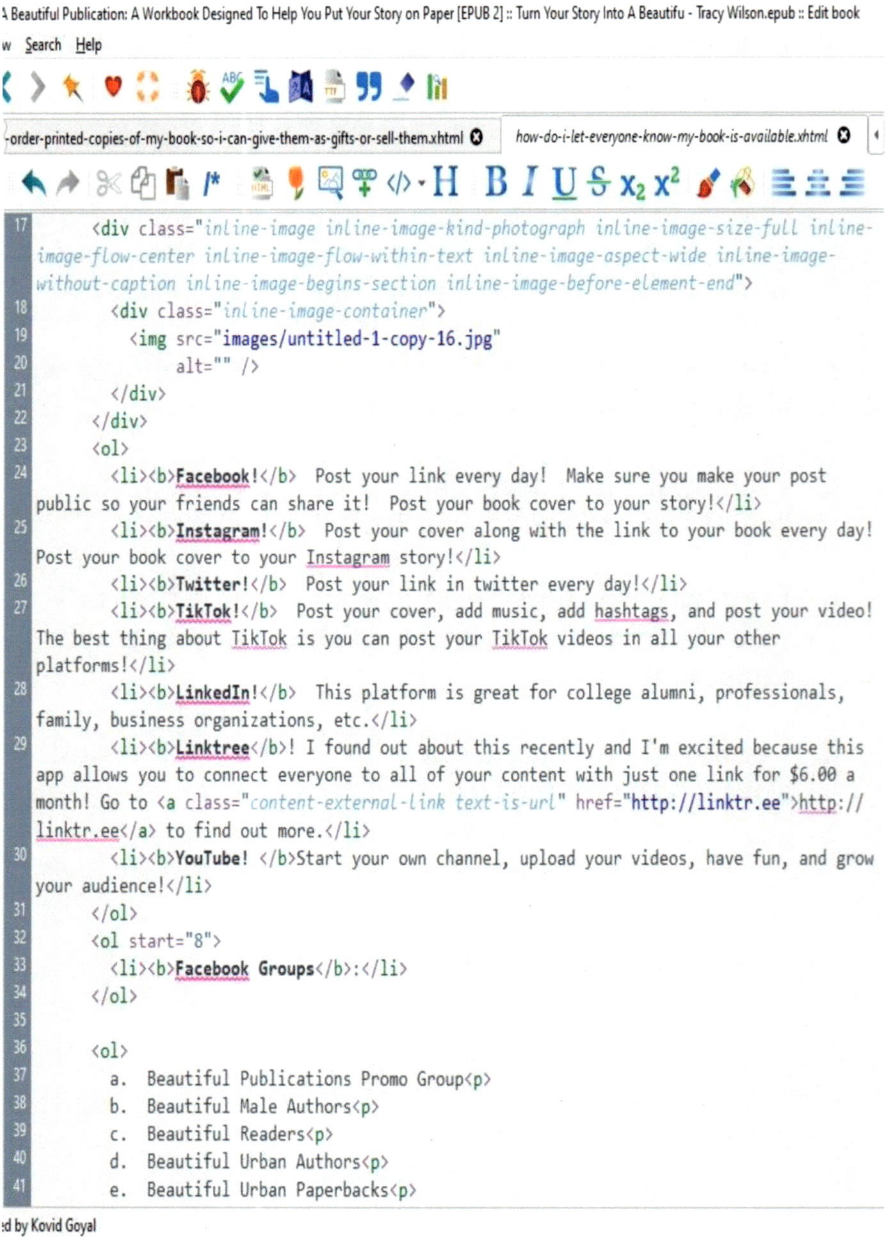

A Beautiful Publication: A Workbook Designed To Help You Put Your Story on Paper [EPUB 2] :: Turn Your Story Into A Beautifu - Tracy Wilson.epub :: Edit book

w Search Help

-order-printed-copies-of-my-book-so-i-can-give-them-as-gifts-or-sell-them.xhtml

how-do-i-let-everyone-know-my-book-is-available.xhtml

```
      <div class="inline-image inline-image-kind-photograph inline-image-size-full inline-image-flow-center inline-image-flow-within-text inline-image-aspect-wide inline-image-without-caption inline-image-begins-section inline-image-before-element-end">
        <div class="inline-image-container">
          <img src="images/untitled-1-copy-16.jpg"
               alt="" />
        </div>
      </div>
      <ol>
        <li><b>Facebook!</b>  Post your link every day!  Make sure you make your post public so your friends can share it!  Post your book cover to your story!</li>
        <li><b>Instagram!</b>  Post your cover along with the link to your book every day! Post your book cover to your Instagram story!</li>
        <li><b>Twitter!</b>  Post your link in twitter every day!</li>
        <li><b>TikTok!</b>  Post your cover, add music, add hashtags, and post your video! The best thing about TikTok is you can post your TikTok videos in all your other platforms!</li>
        <li><b>LinkedIn!</b>  This platform is great for college alumni, professionals, family, business organizations, etc.</li>
        <li><b>Linktree</b>! I found out about this recently and I'm excited because this app allows you to connect everyone to all of your content with just one link for $6.00 a month! Go to <a class="content-external-link text-is-url" href="http://linktr.ee">http://linktr.ee</a> to find out more.</li>
        <li><b>YouTube! </b>Start your own channel, upload your videos, have fun, and grow your audience!</li>
      </ol>
      <ol start="8">
        <li><b>Facebook Groups</b>:</li>
      </ol>

      <ol>
        a.  Beautiful Publications Promo Group<p>
        b.  Beautiful Male Authors<p>
        c.  Beautiful Readers<p>
        d.  Beautiful Urban Authors<p>
        e.  Beautiful Urban Paperbacks<p>
```

:d by Kovid Goyal

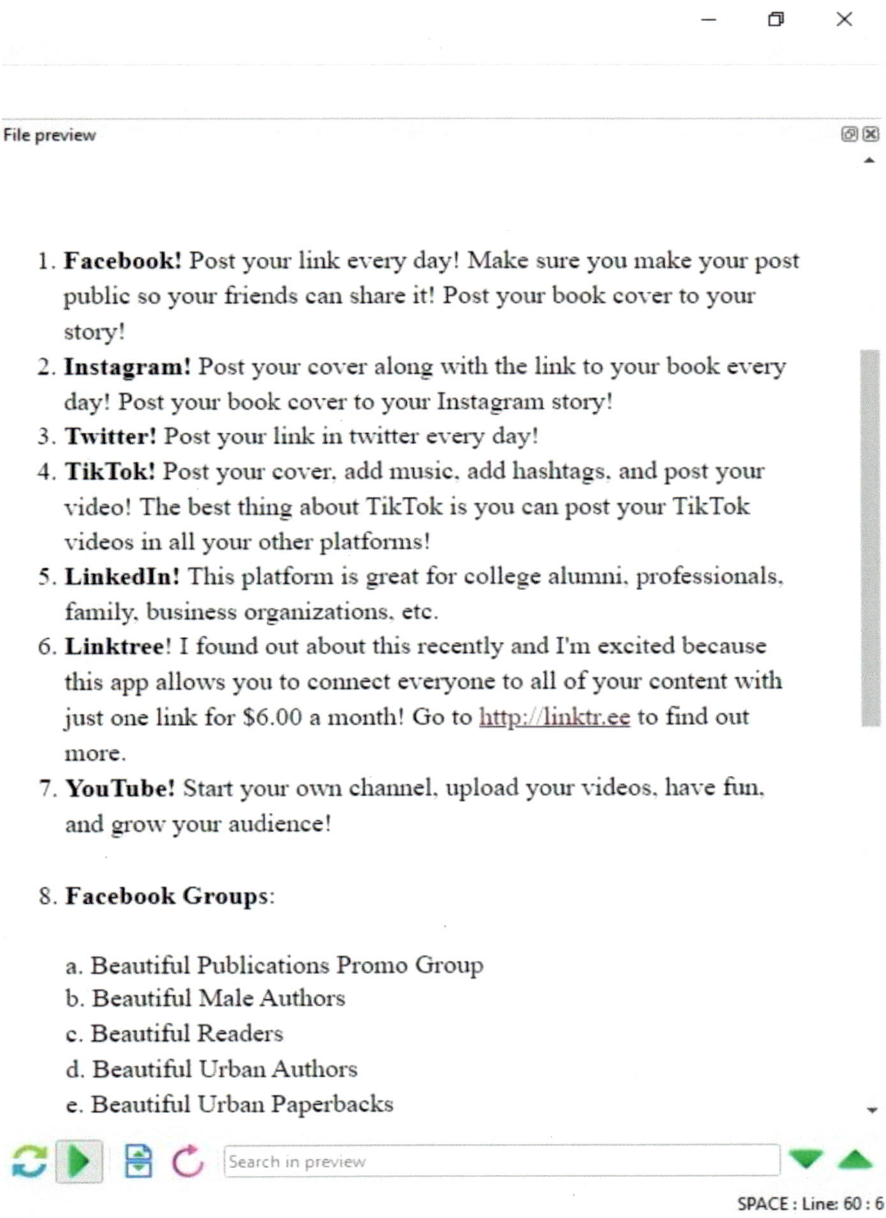

File preview

1. **Facebook!** Post your link every day! Make sure you make your post public so your friends can share it! Post your book cover to your story!
2. **Instagram!** Post your cover along with the link to your book every day! Post your book cover to your Instagram story!
3. **Twitter!** Post your link in twitter every day!
4. **TikTok!** Post your cover, add music, add hashtags, and post your video! The best thing about TikTok is you can post your TikTok videos in all your other platforms!
5. **LinkedIn!** This platform is great for college alumni, professionals, family, business organizations, etc.
6. **Linktree**! I found out about this recently and I'm excited because this app allows you to connect everyone to all of your content with just one link for $6.00 a month! Go to http://linktr.ee to find out more.
7. **YouTube!** Start your own channel, upload your videos, have fun, and grow your audience!

8. **Facebook Groups**:

   a. Beautiful Publications Promo Group
   b. Beautiful Male Authors
   c. Beautiful Readers
   d. Beautiful Urban Authors
   e. Beautiful Urban Paperbacks

Search in preview

SPACE : Line: 60 : 6

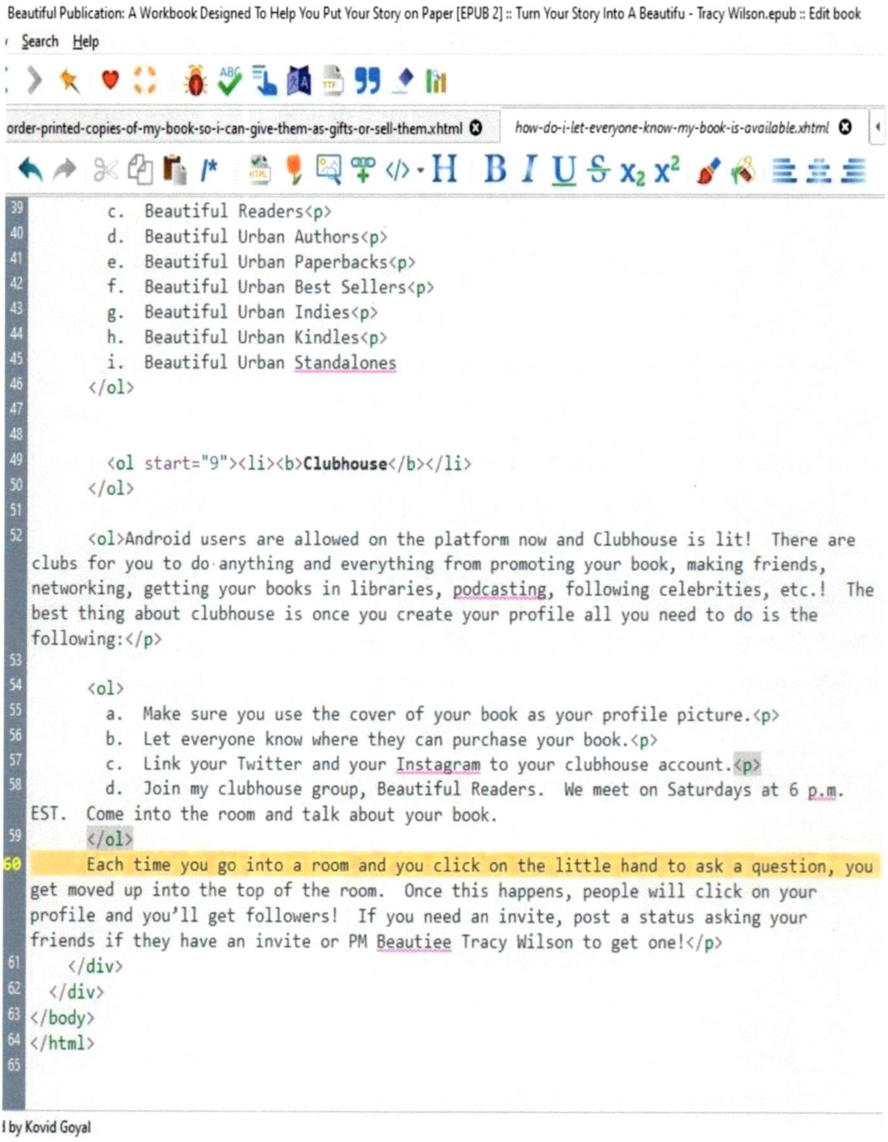


```
        c.  Beautiful Readers<p>
        d.  Beautiful Urban Authors<p>
        e.  Beautiful Urban Paperbacks<p>
        f.  Beautiful Urban Best Sellers<p>
        g.  Beautiful Urban Indies<p>
        h.  Beautiful Urban Kindles<p>
        i.  Beautiful Urban Standalones
      </ol>


        <ol start="9"><li><b>Clubhouse</b></li>
      </ol>

      <ol>Android users are allowed on the platform now and Clubhouse is lit!  There are clubs for you to do anything and everything from promoting your book, making friends, networking, getting your books in libraries, podcasting, following celebrities, etc.!  The best thing about clubhouse is once you create your profile all you need to do is the following:</p>

      <ol>
        a.  Make sure you use the cover of your book as your profile picture.<p>
        b.  Let everyone know where they can purchase your book.<p>
        c.  Link your Twitter and your Instagram to your clubhouse account.<p>
        d.  Join my clubhouse group, Beautiful Readers.  We meet on Saturdays at 6 p.m. EST.  Come into the room and talk about your book.
      </ol>
      Each time you go into a room and you click on the little hand to ask a question, you get moved up into the top of the room.  Once this happens, people will click on your profile and you'll get followers!  If you need an invite, post a status asking your friends if they have an invite or PM Beautiee Tracy Wilson to get one!</p>
    </div>
  </div>
</body>
</html>
```

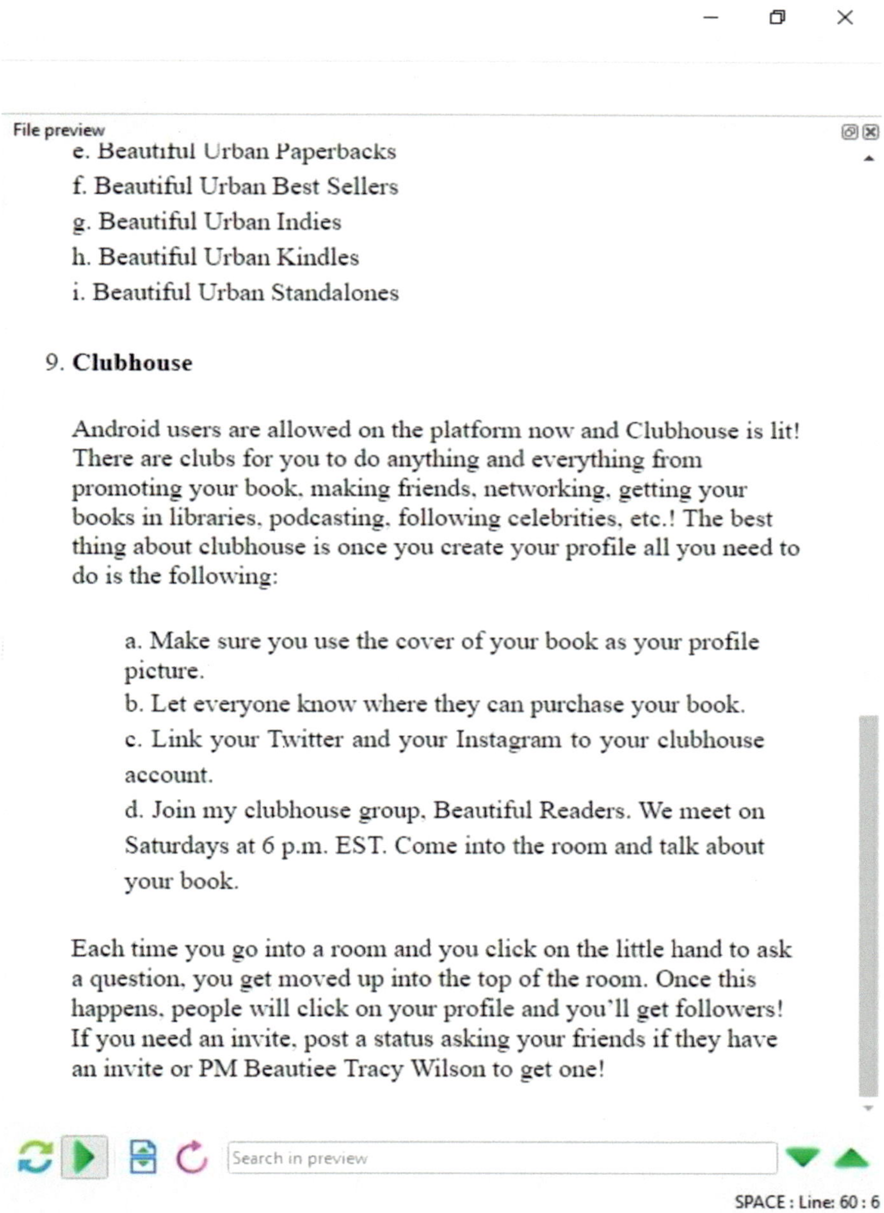

e. Beautiful Urban Paperbacks
f. Beautiful Urban Best Sellers
g. Beautiful Urban Indies
h. Beautiful Urban Kindles
i. Beautiful Urban Standalones

9. **Clubhouse**

Android users are allowed on the platform now and Clubhouse is lit! There are clubs for you to do anything and everything from promoting your book, making friends, networking, getting your books in libraries, podcasting, following celebrities, etc.! The best thing about clubhouse is once you create your profile all you need to do is the following:

a. Make sure you use the cover of your book as your profile picture.
b. Let everyone know where they can purchase your book.
c. Link your Twitter and your Instagram to your clubhouse account.
d. Join my clubhouse group, Beautiful Readers. We meet on Saturdays at 6 p.m. EST. Come into the room and talk about your book.

Each time you go into a room and you click on the little hand to ask a question, you get moved up into the top of the room. Once this happens, people will click on your profile and you'll get followers! If you need an invite, post a status asking your friends if they have an invite or PM Beautiee Tracy Wilson to get one!

When I got to 'I Just Want To Write My Book' I saw the following:

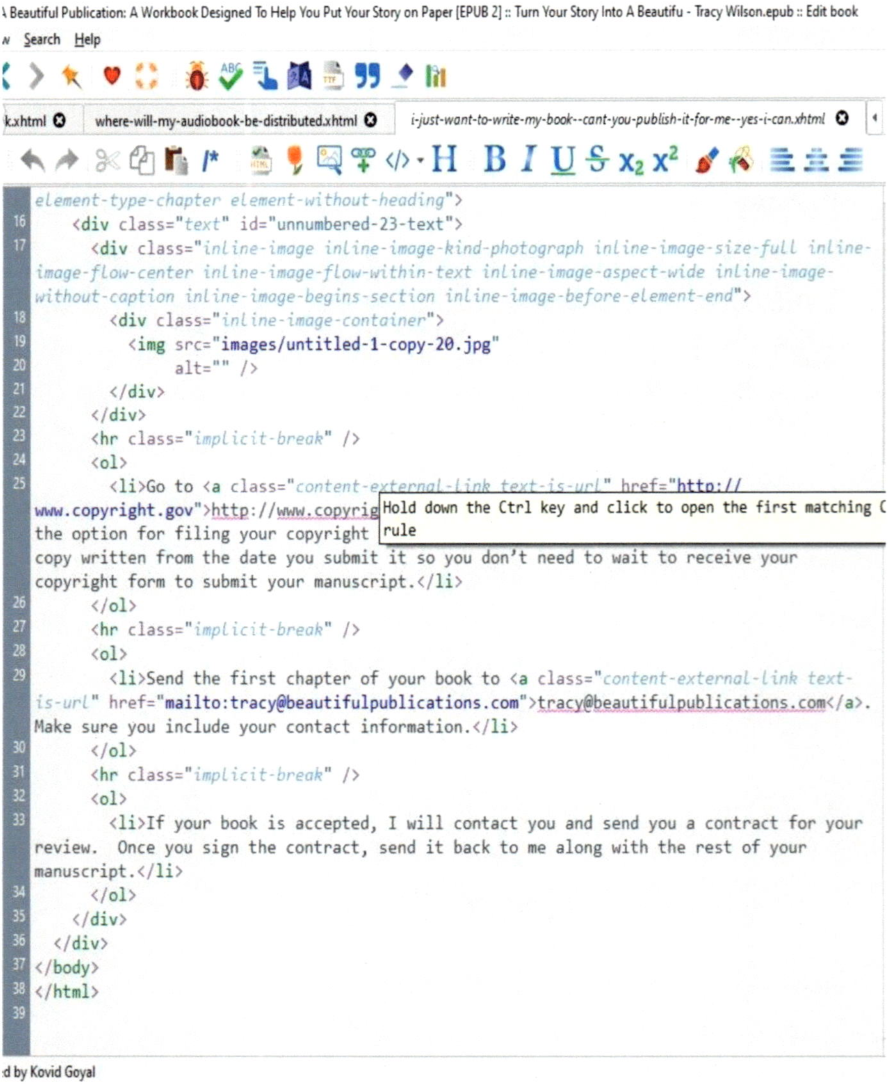

File preview

1. Go to http://www.copyright.gov and fill out the Literary Form TX, or use the option for filing your copyright online and upload your style ook for $65.00. Your book is copy written from the date you submit so you don't need to wait to receive your copyright form to submit your manuscript.

1. Send the first chapter of your book to tracy@beautifulpublications.com. Make sure you include your contact information.

1. If your book is accepted, I will contact you and send you a contract for your review. Once you sign the contract, send it back to me along with the rest of your manuscript.

Search in preview

Line: 1 : 0

1. I changed <ol> to <ol start="1">, <ol start="2">, and <ol start="3"> in front of each paragraph.

2. I removed <hr class="implicit-break" /> after the first and second paragraphs.

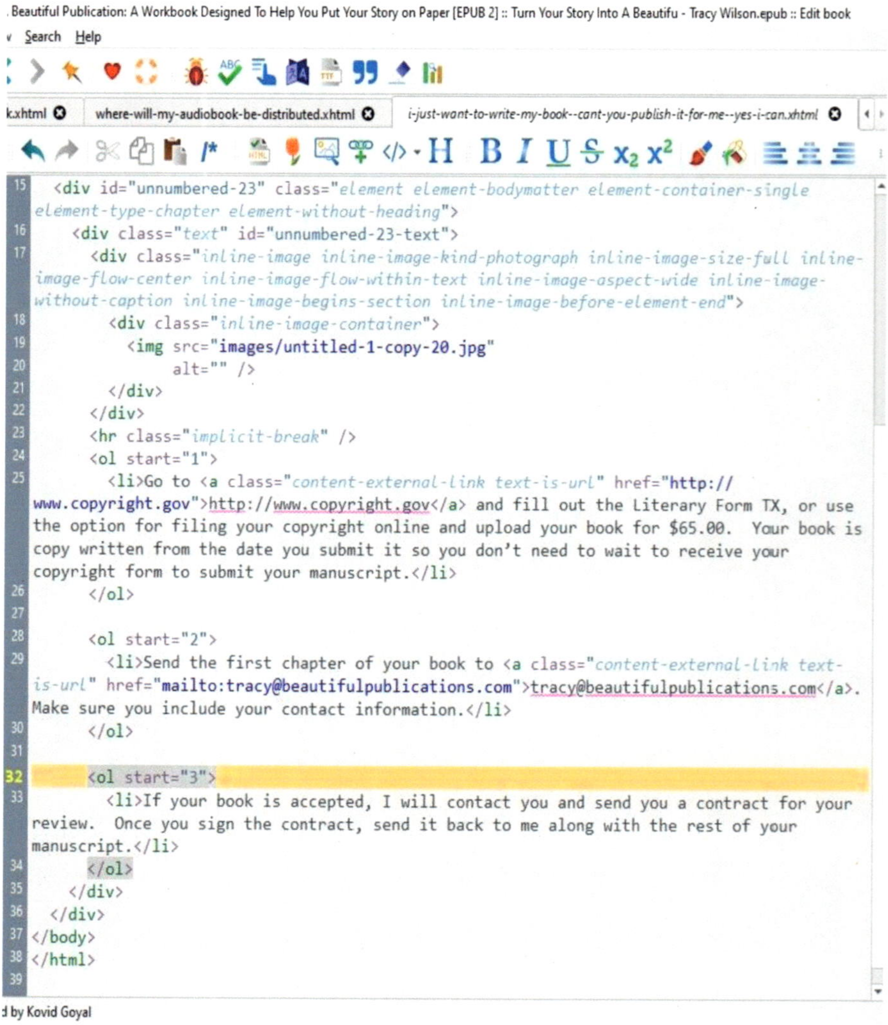


```
  <div id="unnumbered-23" class="element element-bodymatter element-container-single element-type-chapter element-without-heading">
    <div class="text" id="unnumbered-23-text">
      <div class="inline-image inline-image-kind-photograph inline-image-size-full inline-image-flow-center inline-image-flow-within-text inline-image-aspect-wide inline-image-without-caption inline-image-begins-section inline-image-before-element-end">
        <div class="inline-image-container">
          <img src="images/untitled-1-copy-20.jpg"
               alt="" />
        </div>
      </div>
      <hr class="implicit-break" />
      <ol start="1">
        <li>Go to <a class="content-external-link text-is-url" href="http://www.copyright.gov">http://www.copyright.gov</a> and fill out the Literary Form TX, or use the option for filing your copyright online and upload your book for $65.00.  Your book is copy written from the date you submit it so you don't need to wait to receive your copyright form to submit your manuscript.</li>
      </ol>

      <ol start="2">
        <li>Send the first chapter of your book to <a class="content-external-link text-is-url" href="mailto:tracy@beautifulpublications.com">tracy@beautifulpublications.com</a>. Make sure you include your contact information.</li>
      </ol>

      <ol start="3">
        <li>If your book is accepted, I will contact you and send you a contract for your review.  Once you sign the contract, send it back to me along with the rest of your manuscript.</li>
      </ol>
    </div>
  </div>
</body>
</html>
```

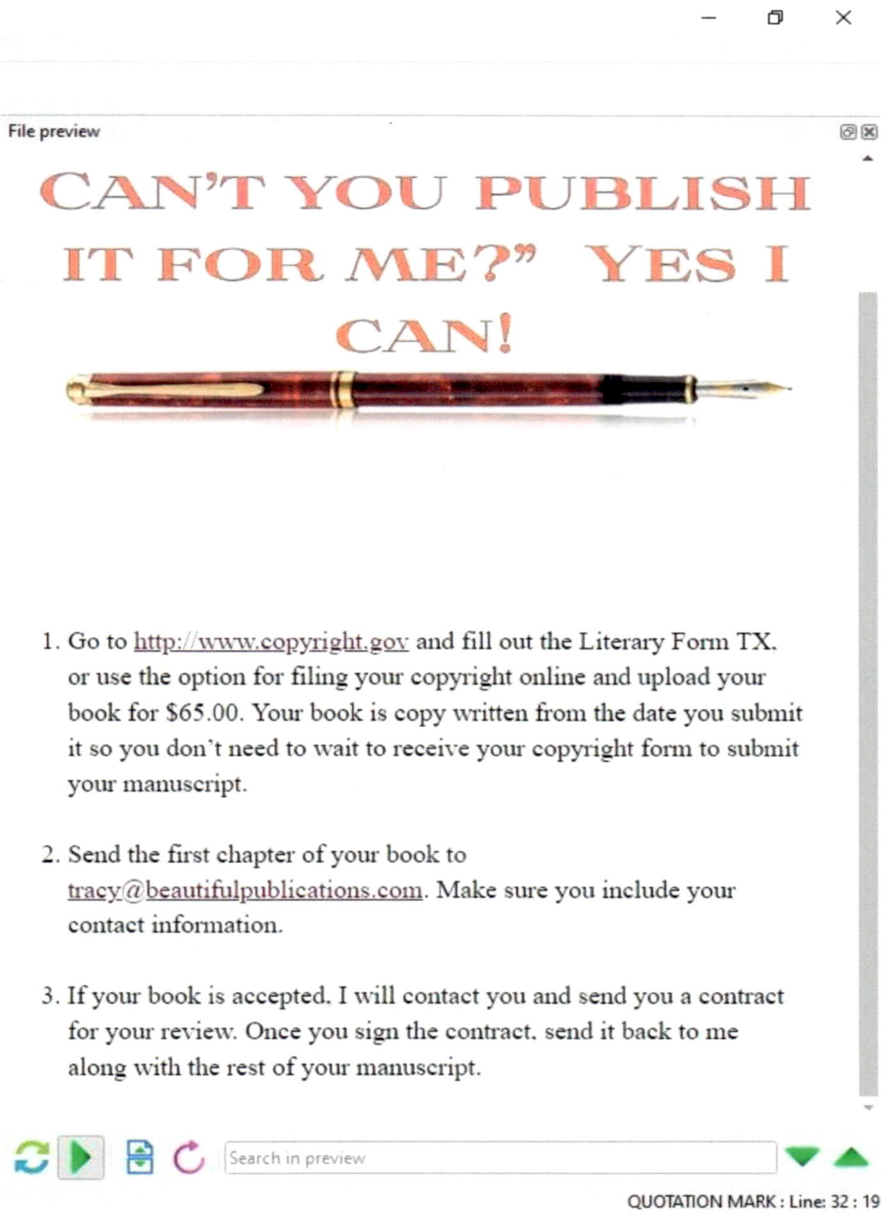

File preview

CAN'T YOU PUBLISH IT FOR ME?" YES I CAN!

1. Go to http://www.copyright.gov and fill out the Literary Form TX, or use the option for filing your copyright online and upload your book for $65.00. Your book is copy written from the date you submit it so you don't need to wait to receive your copyright form to submit your manuscript.

2. Send the first chapter of your book to tracy@beautifulpublications.com. Make sure you include your contact information.

3. If your book is accepted, I will contact you and send you a contract for your review. Once you sign the contract, send it back to me along with the rest of your manuscript.

Search in preview

QUOTATION MARK : Line: 32 : 19

DRAWING TEXT LINES

Now that I was done reading and fixing the html code for my e-book, I wanted to learn how to draw lines on a page for a workbook that was published as an e-book and a paperback, so I googled it, opened up my calibre, added my book, went to 'What's Your Story' and saw the following:

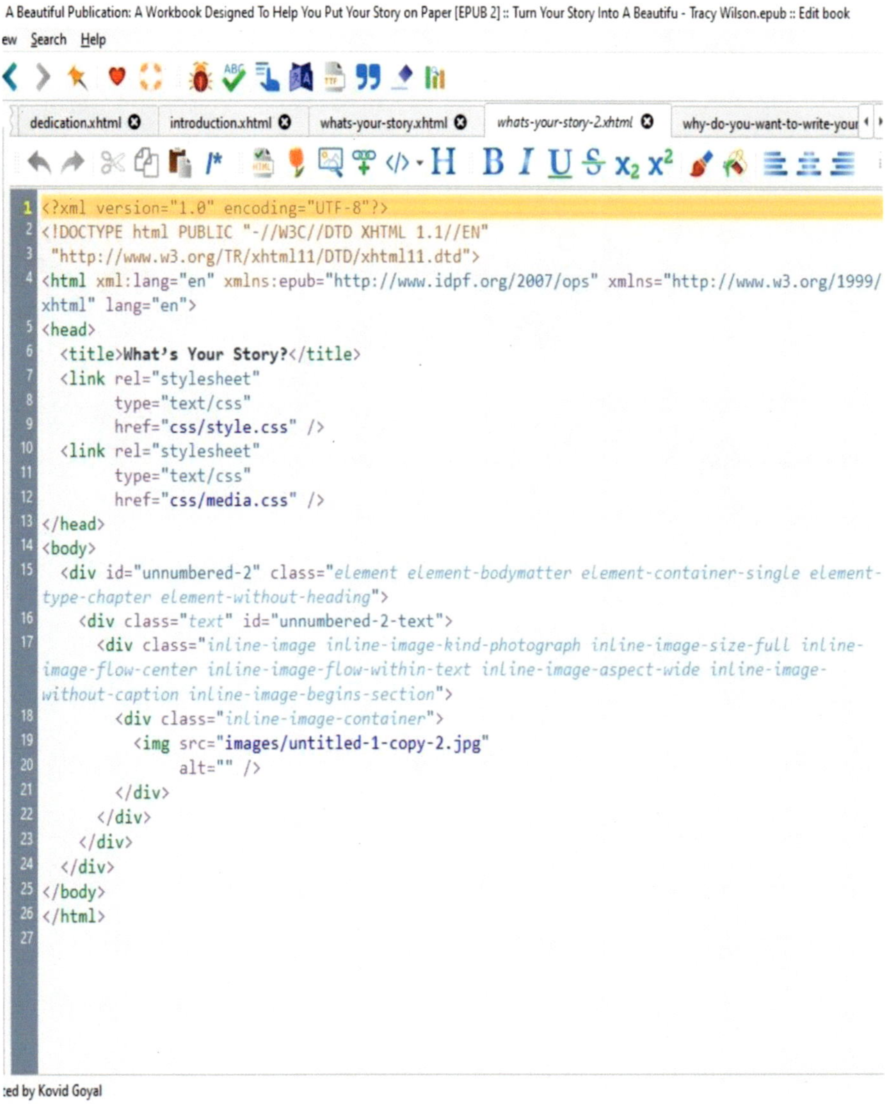


```
<?xml version="1.0" encoding="UTF-8"?>
<!DOCTYPE html PUBLIC "-//W3C//DTD XHTML 1.1//EN"
 "http://www.w3.org/TR/xhtml11/DTD/xhtml11.dtd">
<html xml:lang="en" xmlns:epub="http://www.idpf.org/2007/ops" xmlns="http://www.w3.org/1999/
xhtml" lang="en">
<head>
  <title>What’s Your Story?</title>
  <link rel="stylesheet"
        type="text/css"
        href="css/style.css" />
  <link rel="stylesheet"
        type="text/css"
        href="css/media.css" />
</head>
<body>
  <div id="unnumbered-2" class="element element-bodymatter element-container-single element-
type-chapter element-without-heading">
    <div class="text" id="unnumbered-2-text">
      <div class="inline-image inline-image-kind-photograph inline-image-size-full inline-
image-flow-center inline-image-flow-within-text inline-image-aspect-wide inline-image-
without-caption inline-image-begins-section">
        <div class="inline-image-container">
          <img src="images/untitled-1-copy-2.jpg"
               alt="" />
        </div>
      </div>
    </div>
  </div>
</body>
</html>
```

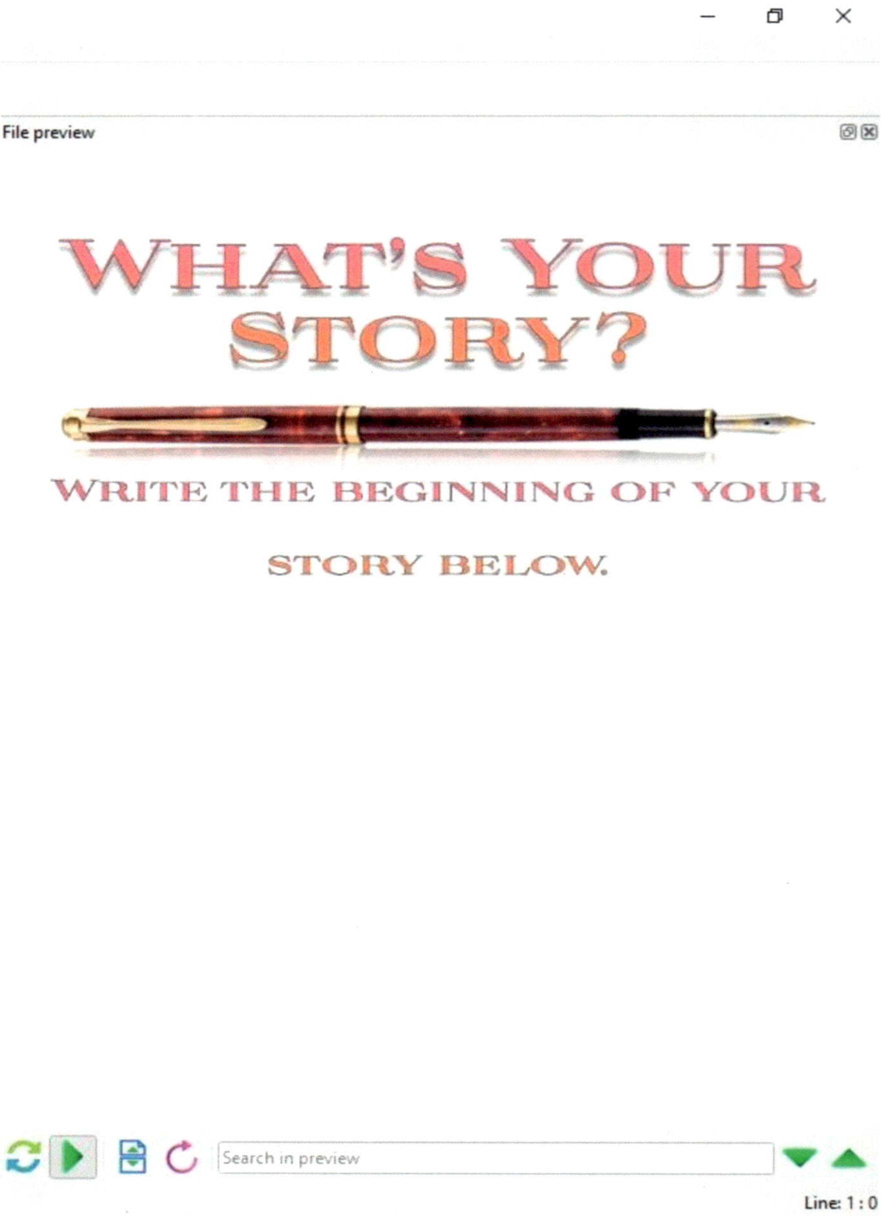
File preview
WHAT'S YOUR STORY?
WRITE THE BEGINNING OF YOUR
STORY BELOW.
Search in preview
Line: 1 : 0

You can draw black lines for text in your e-book using either one of the following html codes:

1.
<hr size ="4" width = 90% color = "rgb(0, 0, 0)"></hr></div>.

2.
<hr size ="4" width = 90% color = "black"></hr></div>.

You can make your lines thicker if you want by changing the size from “4” to “5”

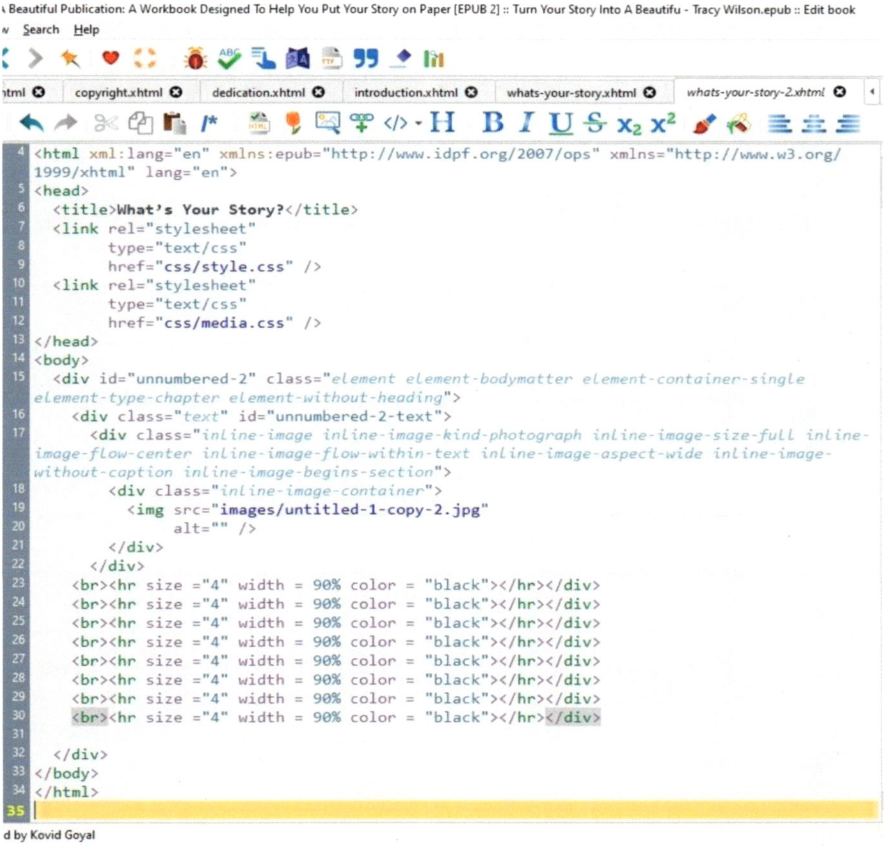


```
<html xml:lang="en" xmlns:epub="http://www.idpf.org/2007/ops" xmlns="http://www.w3.org/1999/xhtml" lang="en">
<head>
  <title>What’s Your Story?</title>
  <link rel="stylesheet"
        type="text/css"
        href="css/style.css" />
  <link rel="stylesheet"
        type="text/css"
        href="css/media.css" />
</head>
<body>
  <div id="unnumbered-2" class="element element-bodymatter element-container-single element-type-chapter element-without-heading">
    <div class="text" id="unnumbered-2-text">
      <div class="inline-image inline-image-kind-photograph inline-image-size-full inline-image-flow-center inline-image-flow-within-text inline-image-aspect-wide inline-image-without-caption inline-image-begins-section">
        <div class="inline-image-container">
          <img src="images/untitled-1-copy-2.jpg"
               alt="" />
        </div>
      </div>
    <br><hr size ="4" width = 90% color = "black"></hr></div>
    <br><hr size ="4" width = 90% color = "black"></hr></div>
    <br><hr size ="4" width = 90% color = "black"></hr></div>
    <br><hr size ="4" width = 90% color = "black"></hr></div>
    <br><hr size ="4" width = 90% color = "black"></hr></div>
    <br><hr size ="4" width = 90% color = "black"></hr></div>
    <br><hr size ="4" width = 90% color = "black"></hr></div>
    <br><hr size ="4" width = 90% color = "black"></hr></div>

  </div>
</body>
</html>
```

File preview
WHAT'S YOUR STORY?
WRITE THE BEGINNING OF YOUR
STORY BELOW.
Search in preview
PARAGRAPH SEPARATOR : Line: 34 : 0

AFTERWORD

I hope this book took away some of your frustration, alleviated your headache, and taught you how to read html code.

Made in the USA
Monee, IL
05 November 2026

67378941R00052